Why It Is Recommended
That You Buy Two Copies
of This Book

Owning two copies of this book is recommended because it is immensely effective in teaching your friends and family members how to help you beat your brain disorder. I know how difficult it is to get people to understand your disorder. **That is why I have written a special chapter specifically for your friends and family to read.**

This special chapter will not only teach your family and friends how to help you, but it will also inspire them to want to help you. Plus, since most people end up reading the whole book after reading the whole chapter, they will gain a new perspective regarding your brain disorder—mainly, that it a biologically based physical disorder that is treatable, and not a character flaw.

There is also a special chapter written specifically for your doctor (or therapist). I believe it is important for your doctor and therapist to know that you are serious about taking responsibility for your own treatment efforts. Giving them a copy of this book will not only send them this message, it will also show them how you prepare to beat your depression or manic-depression using the three-step formula taught in this book. Guaranteed—your doctor will love it! One of my readers said she gave a copy to her doctor, and four days later her doctor had recommended the book to five other patients.

For less than the price of two movie tickets and popcorn, you can invest in a formula that may lead you to a lifetime of freedom from your symptoms just as it has done for me. If you are serious about beating your brain disorder, **grab a second copy of this book to share with your supporters, doctor, and therapist while still having your own copy to refer to when needed.** Then, share your second copy with as many people in your support network as possible.

Win the Battle

The 3-Step Lifesaving Formula to Conquer Depression and Bipolar Disorder

Bob Olson

with Melissa Olson

Chandler House Press
Worcester, Massachusetts
1999

ISBN 1-886284-31-8

Library of Congress Catalog Card Number 98-74420

First Edition

ABCDEFGHIJK

Published by
Chandler House Press
335 Chandler Street
Worcester, MA 01602
USA

President: Lawrence J. Abramoff

Publisher/Editor-in-Chief: Richard J. Staron

Vice President of Sales: Irene S. Bergman

Editorial/Production Manager: Jennifer J. Goguen

Book & Cover Design: Susan Glinert

Author Photo: Daniel Drinon

Chandler House Press books are available at special discounts for bulk purchases. For more information about how to arrange such purchases, please contact Irene Bergman at Chandler House Press, 335 Chandler Street, Worcester, MA 01602, or call (800) 642-6657, or fax (508) 756-9425, or find us on the World Wide Web at www.tatnuck.com.

Chandler House Press books are distributed to the trade by

National Book Network, Inc.
4720 Boston Way
Lanham, MD 20706
(800) 462-6420

For Melissa

(my silent knight)

Contents

A Word from My Doctor

Bipolar disorder, once a neglected area of psychiatry in the United States, is today well-known as one of the two most significantly debilitating major mental illnesses. The mortality and morbidity of this illness accounts for untold suffering and many premature deaths. Those afflicted have families who are bewildered and often helpless to intervene in the face of this recurrent and chronic disorder. The patient suffers from a range of symptoms which often undermines his ability to function in all areas of life—from schooling to work, to family and social activities. The depressive symptoms include often unbearable levels of emotional suffering. Manic symptoms often disrupt the patient's ability to appreciate the nature of the disorder and cooperate with treatment efforts.

The underlying cause of this pervasive disorder is not known. In recent years, there have been several studies suggesting that a pathological gene and specific chromosome had been implicated in its etiology. Though such reports were probably premature, the underlying biological nature of the disorder rests on data that is well-established by family, twin, and adoption studies showing undeniable heritability. Indeed, it is clear that there is some "chemical imbalance," though we do not know the precise nature of these defects.

Numerous public figures have suffered from this disorder, and may have publicized the nature of their problems in order to encourage others to get professional help. Paradoxically, the disorder is associated with a higher degree of creativity than one would expect to find in the general population, suggesting that effective treatment would have a high payoff: restoring an unusually talented cohort of patients to a more fruitful existence.

Modern psychiatry has more tools than were available in years past when patients were secluded in rooms and institutionalized often for long periods. But with advances of new and effective curative and prophylactic medications came the naive notion that this illness could be easily treated. In many, if not most, cases, this is not true. This serious disorder requires meticulous care on the part of the physician, and courage, discipline, and a strong commitment to regain one's health on the part of the patient and his family.

This book is about the struggles of one person to achieve a better outcome and a better life for himself. He has told his story in a characteristically forthright way, illustrating graphically the vicissitudes, especially the periodicity and the chronicity of his illness. The reader will, I believe, appreciate the bravery he showed in fighting to regain his mental health. This book inspires, as it was meant to do, because it tells a true story of a person, who, assisted and supported by his wife and by others, persisted against heavy odds to achieve relief from his suffering and gain significant restoration of his mental health.

I recommend this story to you, and I am proud to have played a small part in its unfolding.

Phillip L. Isenberg, M.D.
McLean Hospital
Boston, Massachusetts

Part I

There are two parts to this book. Part One is the author's key inspirational message of hope and his three-step lifesaving formula for beating depression and manic-depression. Part Two is the author's most popular collection of individual articles written on the truth about labels, the masks we wear, the mystery of suicide, the trickery of denial, and his final message of hope.

Chapter 1

Introduction

I know of no more encouraging fact than the unquestionable ability of man to elevate his life by a conscious endeavor.

—Henry David Thoreau

Follow Me, I Know the Way

If winning your battle with depression (unipolar disorder) or manic-depression (bipolar disorder) is your goal, then this book is your treasure map for achieving that goal. This map is not based on theory or clinical research. This is a map that was drawn by a patient who walked through the battlefields of both depression and mania. I am that patient, and I am revealing to you the path that led me to freedom from the horrors of my brain disorder (mental illness)—manic-depression.

Whether you suffer from depression alone or mania and depression, my simple three-step lifesaving formula can and will guide you to a treatment that will relieve you from your suffering. Forget everything you now believe about your chances of getting better. Stop listening to the limiting messages of people who have not successfully reached the goals that you wish to reach. Doesn't it make more sense to take directions from a person who has successfully made the journey, than from someone who has never been where you want to go? Let me tell you a story that relates to this idea...

Don't Be Led Astray

When I was in my deepest state of depression, and screaming within myself for help, I finally gave in to my doctor's advice to try a support group. I found one support group for people with depression or manic-depression which met weekly at a nearby hospital, so I decided to give it a try. Unfortunately, I picked the wrong night to go to this particular group.

Due to the large attendance that night, the support group was split into two separate groups. The regular support group leader went with the first group. My wife, Melissa, and I were put with the second group led by two patients. They were regular attendees, and supposedly they knew what they were doing. I quickly found out they had no idea what they were doing.

Being the new guy in the group, the leaders, one male and one female, asked me if I wanted to tell my story. I told them that I had tried several medications over the last few years without any success. The leaders then gave me their advice.

The male leader was admittedly depressed. The female leader was obviously and admittedly manic. Both leaders boldly advised me that my expectations for feeling better were too high. They said that I had to accept that I have a brain disorder, and accept the "fact" that medications or other treatment will only improve my symptoms a little. Both leaders added that they had been treating much longer than I, and they had both accepted that his depression and her manic-depression will only improve to the point where they are now.

Quite frankly, I was steaming mad! Since I was severely depressed, I did not have the energy to argue with these people. I just nodded and let them move on to another person. But when break time came, Melissa and I tore out of there.

The first tragedy in this story is that these two patients leading our group learned to "settle" for feeling a *little* better. The male leader was clearly depressed, and the female leader was clearly manic. Still, both told me that they no longer searched for another treatment that would improve the way they felt. They gave up! They quit! For some reason these two individuals believed that happiness and mental stability were impossible for them to obtain, so they stopped looking for a treatment to help them feel better.

Somehow, somewhere, these two support group leaders "learned" these limiting beliefs that caused them to settle for a state of mental health that gives them pain. I stress the word "learned" because this is how we acquire such beliefs. We learn them from other people.

This is important to recognize because ignorance breeds more ignorance. In other words, these two group leaders may be quitters, but only because they were taught to quit by someone else. I am sure they are not evil people. They are more likely just ignorant people passing along an evil message.

This brings me to **the second tragedy in this story**. While it is sad that these two support group leaders chose to settle for feeling just a *little* better, it is frightful and unacceptable that they tried to influence me and others to do the same. I accept that I will always have manic-depression, but I don't have to let it ruin my life. Anyone who is trying to make people believe otherwise is spreading a false and harmful message.

If I had listened to these two misguided group leaders, I would not have woken up this morning smiling and laughing with Melissa. I would not have noticed how beautiful the whistle of the cardinals sounded in our backyard. My mind would either be too high or too low to be running a successful business that gives me the freedom to write this book day after day. If I had "settled" the way they did, I would not have been free of all manic and depressive symptoms for approximately five years now.

Proof That Your Brain Disorder Is Treatable

I am your proof that depression and manic-depression are treatable. I am your proof that happiness can be yours. I am your proof that control over your emotions and behavior is possible. I am your proof that your brain disorder does not have to be your disability, but instead can be a mere obstacle which you can overcome.

I am a living, walking, talking example of what you can do. All you must do now is ignore all the limiting beliefs that you have acquired over the years and take my hand throughout this book to explore your *true* potential for feeling better.

When Sir Isaac Newton discovered gravity because an apple fell on his head, did he have to wait until every apple in the world fell on his head before he believed in his discovery? Certainly not. There are universal laws of nature that govern all things. Well, the same is true for depression and manic-depression. *Millions of patients have successfully been treated for these brain disorders.* It is illogical to think that your case is any different. If you have been correctly diagnosed, then your disorder is treatable. Period!

Depression and manic-depression are caused by a chemical imbalance in the brain. Balance out those chemicals, and the symptoms disappear. That is the universal law that controls these brain disorders. Notice I did not say that the disorder necessarily disappears. In my case, the disorder is hereditary. I still have the brain disorder, but I control it with medication. Fine with me. All I have to do is take a pill each day, and I'm more normal than normal people. My chemicals are now balanced. It's a small price to pay to be free from such a disabling disorder.

Just like when your car starts running poorly, and you need a mechanic to repair it, you never question whether or not the problem can be repaired. Your only concern is how long will it take and how much will it cost. The same should be true for your depression or manic-depression.

How Long Will It Take?

So how long will it take? Just like the car repair, the problem must first be diagnosed. That is what labels are all about. After listening to your list of symptoms, your doctor has diagnosed (labeled) you with depression or manic-depression. All this label means is that you have a particular group of symptoms. This label now helps your doctor determine what treatment will best relieve you of these symptoms, based on the medical community's experience with other patients who have had similar symptoms. Remember this next time you start to think of yourself as "mentally ill" or "manic-depressive." That label is not who you are. It's just a word that categorizes your list of symptoms.

Knowing how long it will take to fix your car or brain disorder is difficult to predict. Ask any mechanic or doctor, and they will tell you the same thing— they are only guessing based on what they know. Every car is different. Some are newer, some older. Some have stronger engines, some weaker. The same is true for people. We are all a bit different. For some, Lithium will work immediately. Others may need an antidepressant, too. Still others are so imbalanced that they may need electroconvulsive therapy to balance out those chemicals.

Nobody knows how long it will take to find the right treatment for you. The good news is that once you find it, your suffering is over. There are so many

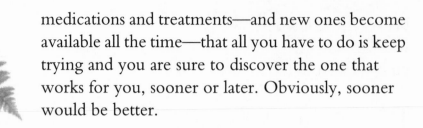

medications and treatments—and new ones become available all the time—that all you have to do is keep trying and you are sure to discover the one that works for you, sooner or later. Obviously, sooner would be better.

How Much Will It Cost?

How much will it cost? This is the same as asking what price you'll have to pay. For the car repair, we are only talking about money. For your mental health, we are talking more about what you'll have to pay *in effort* than what you'll have to pay in dollars.

For instance, you may have to take a pill every day like I do. You might have to take a couple different pills. You may even need electroconvulsive therapy (also known as electroshock treatments). I did. You'll read later how I had twenty-one shock treatments during my search for the right treatment. That was the price I was willing to pay for mental health. As horrible as that may sound to some people, it was nothing compared to the hell I experienced due to my brain disorder. I would do it all over again, if I had to, for the peace and happiness I now experience every day.

I suspect that you feel the same as I did when I was suffering. The question of "How much effort..." isn't really an issue. All you want to do is feel better. Of course, the effort part is going to be a challenge, but you wouldn't be reading this if you weren't willing to do the work. Is this true? It will be if you put the effort in to finish reading this book.

The Three Steps Revealed

This book is going to talk about three steps for winning your battle against depression and manic-depression. In brief, the first step is simply believing in the possibility that you can and will find a treatment that is successful for you. The second step is taking action in pursuit of finding that successful treatment. Too many patients fail at this stage because they are not willing to pay the price necessary to get better. The third step is to be persistent in your efforts toward mental health. By never giving up, you are sure to find the right treatment for you. It could be the next one you try.

The power behind *Belief—Action—Persistence* is much greater than it's simplicity would lead you to believe. Don't be fooled! The pages that follow will reveal a proven formula that will teach your doctors, nurses, therapists, family members, friends, and *you* how to work as a team to successfully beat your brain disorder. All parties involved will benefit immensely by this life-saving formula. Read it. Learn it. Use it. And by all means share it with everyone affected by your disorder.

Notes about Chapter One

Chapter 2

My Story

You can preach a better sermon with your life than with your lips.

—Oliver Goldsmith

This is a book about getting well. It is not another dreary portrait of a life plagued by mental illness. My story is actually one of inspiration. It has a real life Rocky-type plot that could be made into a fairy tale. The moral of the story is the subject of this book: If you believe you can and will find a treatment to end your suffering, take the necessary action to fulfill that belief, and continue with an unrelenting persistence toward that goal, then you will one day succeed at making that dream come true.

I inherited manic-depression (bipolar disorder) from my father's side of the family, so I lived with periodic mania and depression all my life. As I got older, the intensity of each mania and depression grew worse, as did the length of time of each episode. Before my diagnosis, I never knew I had a brain disorder (mental illness), so it was all quite confusing to me. Eventually the signs became too undeniable to ignore.

I was diagnosed in 1989 at the age of twenty-seven. Diagnosis was quick and easy. Unfortunately, finding a treatment that would work for me was not so easy. It took over fifteen medications (and combinations thereof), three doctors, two ECT specialists, twenty-one shock treatments, and five years to finally locate the treatment that would eliminate my misery.

During this five-year quest, it was not my mania that tormented me as much as my depression. I became more deeply depressed with each never-ending day. After the first year, I could no longer work. By the second year, I rarely left my apartment. Around this time, I was determined to be totally disabled and received four hundred dollars a month from Social Security Disability Insurance. By my third, fourth, and fifth years, I spent an average of eighteen hours a day sleeping.

My wife, Melissa, was wonderful about pushing me to get out of the house on weekends and getting me around other people as much as possible. Still, an average weekday during this time involved: Getting out of bed to drive Melissa to work. Going back home to sleep until lunchtime. Getting out of bed to pick her up for lunch. Going home to sleep until the end of her work day. Getting up once more to pick her up from work. Going back to sleep until supper was ready. Getting up to eat, watch some television with her, and then going back to bed for the night.

Before I go any further, you should understand that it is not the norm to go through five years of hell in order to find a treatment that works. Millions of people have succeeded on their first or second trial. I admit that I was not that lucky. But the point of this book is that I stuck it out, kept trying, and eventually struck oil. I can assure you that it was all worth it.

Many people ask why it took me five years to get well. Nobody knows for sure. It's like playing a slot machine in Vegas. You know you'll hit it big sooner or later. You just don't know if it will be the first med-ication you try or the sixth. For me it was beyond the fifteenth.

I'm going to be talking about persistence in an up-coming chapter, so I'm going to give you an example of what that is now. When I mention that I tried fif-teen medications (or combinations of medications), many people don't have a clue what this means. Let me explain...

When a medication is tried for the first time, many can take three to four weeks to take effect. To be sure whether a medication is helpful or not, my doctors recommended that I give each one at least a three-month trial period. This was true for the Lithium as well as the antidepressants I tried, including the try-cyclics, the MAO Inhibitors, and the second generation antidepressants.

Some medications also required that I wait a week or two to wean off of them before trying something new. So picture this: I begin taking Lithium for sev-eral months. I finally must admit that it isn't working. Now I pick myself up, brush myself off, and try an antidepressant. I get my hopes up that it's going to work, and then a few months later I am disappointed that this one failed, too. With the encouragement of my doctor and wife, I try another antidepressant. At first I think that maybe it's helping, but after about five months I can no longer deny that I'm now more depressed than ever. This scenario continued like a roller coaster that wouldn't stop for five years. Of course, I always could have got off that roller coaster by not trying something else, but that would have meant having to live in the house of horrors—my manic-depressive mind—forever.

Most patients will tell you that taking the pills isn't the problem, it's the side effects that torture you. I must have experienced every side effect known to man at one time or another. One medication made me gain twenty-four pounds in only a few weeks. Another slurred my speech and blurred my vision. Another caused me some hair loss. Still another made me dizzy. Several gave me stomach cramps and problems you don't want me to describe. One medication made my muscles twitch so violently that I sometimes punched and kicked Melissa while sleeping. One even made my teeth numb. Some made my hands shake so badly it was difficult to write. Then there were those that made me sleepy all day, and those that kept me awake all night.

I could continue this list of side effects for another page, but I won't. That would paint a picture that might make it all look worse than it actually was. Except for that sudden weight gain, I really didn't mind all the side effects. I even laughed about some of them. That was a bonus considering my saddened state of mind. You have to admit that a flying arm or leg in the middle of the night is kind of comical—especially when your spouse has to dodge them.

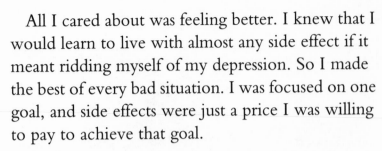

All I cared about was feeling better. I knew that I would learn to live with almost any side effect if it meant ridding myself of my depression. So I made the best of every bad situation. I was focused on one goal, and side effects were just a price I was willing to pay to achieve that goal.

Well, it came to the point where I had tried every category of medication available at that time. New ones were coming out, but were not yet approved by the Food and Drug Administration. After careful consideration, and an interview with an ECT (electroconvulsive therapy) specialist, it was decided that electroshock treatments were the next logical step.

Although most people shudder at the thought of going through ECT, I welcomed it. I was in great pain and had been tempted by the thought of suicide for years. I had told my doctors at the time that suicide was not a concern, but I had put a gun to my head more than once. If it were not for my love for Melissa, I might not be here today. Even in my darkest moments, I could not be so selfish as to hurt her for my own escape. So ECT was no threat to me. I would have allowed myself to be tarred and feathered if someone told me it might put an end to my suffering.

The ECT doctor said I might feel a difference after just a few shock treatments. Still, he added that it can take several treatments before some patients notice any results. By my fourteenth treatment I was losing hope that it would work at all. Over six weeks of

ECT treatments had passed, and I was still begging I might die in my sleep. It was at this time that Melissa's health insurance was changing, and I would soon have to change doctors altogether.

With the new health insurance came the opportunity to find a new doctor at one of the best hospitals for mental illness in the country—McLean Hospital in Belmont, Massachusetts. Not that I disliked my previous doctors, but it was reassuring to get another opinion regarding my case. Every doctor I had previously seen suggested that I might be "medication resistant." So far all evidence led in that direction. Nonetheless, my new doctor agreed that I was on the right path, so we continued with additional shock treatments.

After additional ECT, there was still no improvement. Since we had only gone with unilateral ECT (one side of my brain) up to this point, we decided to try bilateral ECT (both sides of my brain). After just four bilateral treatments, I decided to go no further. The bilateral treatments had caused me some disturbing, although temporary, memory loss; and I had seen no positive results. After a total of twenty-one shock treatments with no success, it made almost no sense to continue.

This was a critical point in my life. It had been five years since I was first diagnosed and began treatment with medication. After fifteen medications and twenty-one shock treatments, I had made no progress. In fact, I had gotten worse. I had tried every available

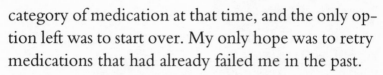

category of medication at that time, and the only option left was to start over. My only hope was to retry medications that had already failed me in the past.

So that's what I did. I tried one medication again. It didn't work. Then I tried another medication for a second time...

After all we had been through together, Melissa and I had to dig deep to find the remaining sparks of hope within our souls. Trying a medication that had already failed to work didn't give us much reason to celebrate, but we still both believed this nightmare would end some day. Thank God we never gave up.

On the seventh day of taking that pill, I woke up to a gorgeous sunny day. Melissa was going to a wedding that day without me. Even though the wedding was for a cousin on my side of the family, Melissa was used to going to family gatherings without me. By this time, it was rare that I ever left the house for any social event.

I knew I was feeling pretty good that morning, so I told Melissa that I would go to the ceremony with her, and then she could stay through the reception without me. However, to our surprise, when the ceremony was over, I was still feeling happy and sociable. I decided to stick around during the reception for a while since I could always go home later if the depression returned. Well, I never did go home. Instead I talked with family and friends, I joked and laughed, I played games, and I smiled effortlessly all day.

Melissa and I were careful not to jump to any conclusions. We waited to see how I'd feel the next day. We were conditioned not to get too excited, fearing that disappointment may soon follow. That never happened. As each day passed, I felt even better.

Within two months I found a job and began working full-time (for the first time in almost four years). Within five months I started my own business on the side. Finally, only ten months after I began feeling better, I was working full-time running my own successful business. Today, contrary to a few pessimists' predictions that my relief was only temporary, it has been about five years of nothing less than magical bliss.

My doctor from McLean Hospital retired less than a year after we won that battle against my brain disorder. He told me that in all his years of practice, I was his most successful case. When I asked him what made my case so special, he said it was a perfect example of the value of persistence. He not only commended Melissa and me for our inner strength to never give up in our hope and effort, but he was equally impressed with the persistent vision and support of the doctors that came before him. I could not have said it better, except that I would certainly have added him to that list of heroes who helped save my life.

Notes about Chapter Two

Chapter 3

Belief

The only thing that stands between man and what he wants from life is often merely the will to try it and the faith to believe that it is possible.

—Richard M. De Vos

Our Beliefs Create Our Reality

When I was in my late teens, I used to make extra money by cleaning rain gutters on the roofs of houses. One Saturday morning, as I started the day with my first house, I accidentally kicked my ladder as I climbed onto the roof. The ladder slid sideways and down to the ground. There was nobody home at the house and no nearby neighbors, so I sat on the roof waiting for someone to rescue me.

Seven hours later the homeowner returned. When I yelled down to her explaining my predicament, she looked up at me and shouted, "Why didn't you just use the painter's ladder that he left leaning against the back of the house?"

The second my ladder fell that morning, I panicked. All I could imagine was that I might be stuck up on that roof for hours. I didn't believe that there was another ladder leaning against the back of the house, so I never even walked back there to look. Therefore, what I believed would happen became true: I sat up on that roof for hours.

Sometimes the solutions to our problems in life are just around the corner. All we have to do is stop believing that bad things will happen, and start believing there are possible solutions. I believed I was stuck on that roof, so that became my reality. If instead I had believed I could find a way off, I would have made the effort to look for a solution. In less than one minute my problem would have been solved.

If you are suffering from depression or manic-depression, then you must believe there is a solution to end your suffering. If all you are doing is believing that your life sucks and imagining a desperate future, then you are sitting on the front of that roof with a ladder waiting in the back. There are countless treatment possibilities that could balance out those mixed up chemicals in your brain. The first secret to finding the right treatment is **believing that you will find it.**

A Belief in Hope Can Save Your Life

When I talk about "believing that you will get better," I'm talking about something that is as important to the human mind as water is to the human body. I'm talking about *hope*. During my years of depression, I'm sure I could have lived for weeks without water, but I doubt I would have lasted a day without hope.

This, of course, leads to the subject that nobody wants to hear about: suicide. Unfortunately, ignoring the subject won't make it go away. In fact, ignoring it only encourages it—much like ignoring worn brakes on your car. Neither problem is going to fix itself, and ignoring either one could be fatal. So let's take a moment to inspect this problem.

I know from experience that suicide can result from the loss of hope. I have heard people refer to suicide as "a cry for help." What suicidal patients actually need *help* with is finding some *hope*. They have run out of solutions to their problems, and have no hope of finding a new one.

My own experience taught me that I did not need anyone to *fix* my problems to prevent my suicidal impulses. I only needed help seeing a light at the end of the tunnel. Give me hope that my problems can and will be solved, and that will give me the strength to continue fighting.

This reminds me of a young man I met while I was still depressed. He was another patient suffering from depression. He also suffered from alcoholism.

This young man's father was trying to be supportive. He found his son a job, bought him a car, and let him live at home rent-free. When the young man was arrested for drunk driving, the father pulled some strings and got the case dismissed. Three months later, the young man committed suicide.

The father is not to blame. He did everything he knew how to do to fix his son's problems. He should be praised just for trying. Unfortunately, painting the house won't strengthen the weak foundation. Everything may look pretty from the outside, but the inside is still suffering.

What the father didn't know was that his son also needed help fighting his illnesses. His father's support in this way may have given the young man enough hope in his future to keep fighting. Instead, he took his life because he believed his future was hopeless. He saw no end to his suffering.

I trust that you are beginning to see the incredible power of belief. Don't forget that its power can work both for you and against you. A belief that you will win, will *lead* you to that result. A belief that you will lose, will *limit* you to that result. So all you have to do is remain hopeful by believing that you will win; but how do you do that?

Beliefs Gain Strength in Numbers

No battle was ever won by one person alone. I'm sorry, but even John Wayne and Clint Eastwood had help fighting their battles in the movies. They always came out as the heroes, but they didn't do it alone. The same is true for your battle against depression or manic-depression.

I'd like to think that I was strong enough to have won my battle against manic-depression all on my own, but that just isn't the truth. Just like you, I needed people to help me remain hopeful. I needed people to help me believe that despite all the time that had passed, and all the treatments that had failed, happiness was right around the corner.

In addition to my wife, Melissa, the most important people in my life during my depression were my doctors. Not only because they were trying to find ways to help me, but more importantly, because they kept both of us believing that help was possible. From the day of my diagnosis, until the day I got better five years later, my doctors skillfully navigated my belief toward the possibility of success.

On the day of my diagnosis, my doctor assured me that, due to medical breakthroughs in the last ten years, millions of patients with manic-depressive illness lead ordinary lives free from its roller-coaster-like symptoms. She suggested I try Lithium. So with an optimistic attitude, I began treatment.

Months later, when it was obvious that the Lithium did not help, my doctor showed no dismay. She told me that a large number of people who don't respond to Lithium have great success with antidepressants. Before I ever had time to focus on the failure of Lithium, I was already looking forward to trying an antidepressant.

By the time this second medication had failed me, I had recently been assigned to a different doctor. This second doctor was even more encouraging than my first. This guy was enthusiastic about his job. With childlike excitement, he explained the many types of medications that were available to me. He suggested which one I should try next, and he explained why that made sense. By the time my first appointment with him was over, I was convinced that with all the possible medications that existed, my problem was not if I would find one that worked; but rather, when I would find it. This doctor's ability to keep this belief in my mind kept me fighting for over three years.

It was not as if my doctors actually gave me a pep talk at every appointment. They merely showed me that my glass was half-full instead of half-empty. They reminded me that every failed treatment brought me one step closer to the one that would work. Later, when I expressed fear that I might run out of things to try, they told me about all the up-and-coming medications that would soon be on the market.

By the time I changed to my third doctor, he had his work cut out for him. It had been over four years by this time. When Melissa's health insurance changed, I switched to him because he and the hospital he worked at came highly recommended. I had tried every type of medication with poor results, and had just finished fourteen electroshock treatments with similar results. I was really hoping he would notice something the other doctors might have missed. The reality was that my prior doctors didn't miss anything.

This third doctor motivated me to continue with additional ECT (electroconvulsive therapy). After more unproductive unilateral ECT, he gave me hope that the bilateral ECT might work. It was when this failed that he proved his true worth. I can only describe what he did next as nothing less than heroic.

As I mentioned in the first chapter, this was a critical time in my life. I had tried all the medications. No new ones would be available for some time. My only option was to begin all over again—trying medications that had already failed me. Both Melissa and I looked to my doctor for a reason to be hopeful.

My doctor showed no signs of defeat. He told us that it was likely that the ECT had a beneficial effect on the chemicals in my brain, even though I did not notice any significant improvements. He said it was possible that my depression may have been too severe for the medications to pull me out of it. Yet, he believed that the ECT may have pulled me out enough for a medication to now be able to finish the job.

You already read in chapter one that my life was renewed by the second medication I tried after ECT. That is the same medication I still take today with total success. I do not know if this doctor actually believed in his theory at the time. All that really matters is that I believed. It was that belief that gave me hope.

In addition to your doctors, your beliefs are influenced by your nurses, therapists, friends, coworkers, and family members. It is vital that you listen to those who give you positive messages, and avoid those who give you negative messages.

Don't Wait for Everyone

Although I know from my own experience that you may feel the need for encouragement from everyone you love, you must recognize that some people are not going to understand your brain disorder. Some can't understand, and some just can't deal with it. Do not let their weakness affect your beliefs.

If you believe that you can get better, then the power of your belief will propel you into action that will bring forth that result. Do not put limits on your ability to heal by waiting for the wrong people to support you. By simply taking *action* toward your goal, you will find the people who are best suited to help you reach it, which leads us to the next chapter...

Notes about Chapter Three

Chapter 4

Action

They always say that time changes things, but you actually have to change them yourself.

—Andy Warhol

God Helps Those Who Help Themselves

There is an old joke that describes a man who was down on his luck financially. He was a religious man, so he had faith that God would help him. Every morning and every night the man would pray to God for help to win the lottery. For forty years this faithful man continued these daily prayers while living in total poverty.

When the man died and went to heaven, he was quite angry. "Why did you let me down?" he asked God. "I had faith that you would let me win the lottery! I prayed to you every morning and every night!" he cried.

God shrugged his shoulders and replied, "I heard all your prayers. For forty years I wanted to help you, but you never bought a lottery ticket."

I guess that even God can't help us until we take action to help ourselves.

My lottery tickets for winning my battle against manic-depression were my treatments. I played those tickets every day for five years. Finally, the medication that made me feel better became my winning ticket.

This chapter is about *action*. It is the next step of my three-step lifesaving formula known as *Belief— Action—Persistence*. The man described in that old

joke had a strong belief that he would win the lottery. Yet, he didn't win because he never made the
effort to buy a lottery ticket.

As you can see, even a strong belief that you will win
your battle against depression or manic-depression is
not enough. You have to take the necessary action to
find a treatment that works for you.

The Choice of Your Lifetime

If you were lost and all alone in a huge forest, you
would have two choices of what to do. First, you could
sit under a tree waiting for help. Second, you
could pull out your map, determine the most logical
way out, and start walking in that direction while
yelling for help. Which choice do you think is more
likely to save you?

Depression and manic-depression are a lot like
being lost in a huge forest. If you are just waiting for
your illness to go away, then you have made the first
choice described above. If you have gone to a doctor
for help, and are working *with* your doctor trying
various ways to treat your illness, then you have
made the second choice.

Notice that I wrote, "working with your doctor,"
as opposed to, "letting your doctor do all the work."
Your doctor can't help you unless you are willing to
follow his instructions. He knows the way out of the

forest, but he isn't going to carry you out. He can only guide you. You have to do the work.

That is how I found my way out of the forest. I knew my doctors held the map that revealed the best routes out of my manic-depression. They suggested the most logical treatments to try, and I followed their instructions. Some trails led me back to where I started, but there were plenty of new trails to try. Eventually, with my doctors' guidance and my effort, I found my way out of the woods.

The Four Basic Actions That Worked for Me

*The first way I worked with my doctors was by **going to my doctor appointments**.* This meant getting out of bed (not easy with severe depression), showering (also not easy, but doctors really appreciate it), and driving down to their office. This may all seem trivial to you, but many patients are not willing to make this single effort. The bottom line is that your doctor can't help you unless you go to your appointments!!!

*The second way I worked with my doctors was by **following through with my treatments**.* For me, this meant taking my medications and going through my ECT (electroconvulsive therapy). I knew my disorder was caused by a chemical imbalance in my brain. Since I had suffered from the ups and downs of manic-depression for over twenty-seven years, I knew it wouldn't go away on its own. I made the decision that any inconvenience the medications or ECT could cause me would be worth it for the benefit of balancing out those chemicals.

For one reason or another, many patients do not take their medication. You wouldn't expect to win the lottery without buying a lottery ticket. Why would you expect your chemicals to balance out, and then stay balanced, without taking your medication? If you are neglecting to take your medication to gain attention, you will get better results by directly expressing your need for attention. If, however, you are really just absent-minded about taking your medication, then there are several solutions to this problem. You could buy an alarm watch, set an alarm clock, ask a friend to phone you, or tie a string around your finger.

The third way I worked with my doctors was by **learning about my brain disorder**. This involved reading books and articles about manic-depression, as well as finding information about each medication I tried. With this knowledge, it was easier for my doctors to talk to me. Rather than waste precious time trying to explain the basics to me, my doctors could get deeper into the "how and why" of my treatments. This made me feel more comfortable. And since my doctors respected, and often used, my suggestions regarding my treatments, this made me feel more in control.

The fourth way I worked with my doctors was by **learning how to cope with my brain disorder**. The ability to

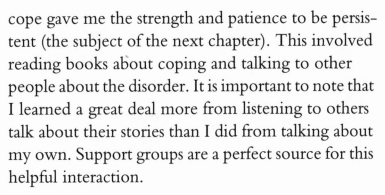

cope gave me the strength and patience to be persistent (the subject of the next chapter). This involved reading books about coping and talking to other people about the disorder. It is important to note that I learned a great deal more from listening to others talk about their stories than I did from talking about my own. Support groups are a perfect source for this helpful interaction.

(Please don't think that my support group experience, mentioned in the introduction of this book, is representative of most support groups. It is not. Most support groups are led by well-qualified individuals. I highly recommend that you join one that makes you feel comfortable).

Another way I helped myself cope was by releasing my emotions through writing. I wrote boxes of articles, poems, and journals which allowed me to express feelings I could not communicate verbally. Some of these writings were shared with people who supported me. Most, however, eased my discomfort solely through the act of writing.

The arts are an invaluable tool for coping with the torment of depression and manic-depression. Whatever type of art works for you, use it. Perhaps you can benefit from writing, dance, photography, painting, music, drawing, sculpture, or crafts. The possibilities are as endless as the relief you can attain.

A Fifth Action That Can Work Miracles

It would be unfair for me to write this chapter on action without validating the value of **spiritual action**. The word "spirituality" means different things to different people. Regardless of your interpretation, your spiritual faith and medical science are the ideal complement to one another. They should not be seen as two opposing alternatives. Instead, they can work together toward the achievement of your goal of mental health.

When I was sick, I prayed for a treatment that would end my suffering. My faith strengthened my *belief* that I would find it. At life's toughest moments, this spiritual action provided me with the necessary hope to continue my efforts toward that goal. In other words, this spiritual *action* reinforced my *belief* which motivated my *persistence*.

As you begin to live by this three-step formula, you will quickly learn that each step assists the other two like members of a team. Belief promotes action— the rewards of *action* increase *belief*—the result is *persistence*—which leads to success.

Simple Efforts Can Bring Unexpected Rewards

I have one last story to share with you about *action*. It is one example of how unexpected help gravitates toward us when we make the effort to help ourselves.

During my depression, I was encouraged to take walks as much as possible because exercise is a proven mood elevator. It was difficult to drum up the energy, but I made the extra effort on beautiful days.

One sunny day I walked so far that I no longer recognized my surroundings. This was just weeks after my bilateral electroshock treatments, so my memory was a bit foggy. Anyway, I was lost. There were plenty of houses around, but I was too embarrassed to ask anyone for directions.

I finally found a highway I recognized, and decided I had no choice but to walk along it toward my home. After a mile or so, I realized I was miles from my exit. I decided to try to find a shortcut through the woods. As I attempted to climb over the fence on the side of the highway, I heard someone yelling to me.

It was a man who was driving his mother to her eye doctor for a checkup. She had recently injured one eye, and wore a black patch over it. With her one eye, this woman had seen me walk by her house earlier, and had mentioned to her son that I looked lost. When they saw me trying to scale the fence by the highway, they were sure of it.

Lucky for me, they pulled over to offer me a ride. The man told me that I was heading for about eighty acres of swampland. If it were not for these two considerate human beings, I would have literally become lost in the forest.

However, this story does not end here. As the man and his mother drove me home, they asked me how I became so lost. I briefly surrendered the story about my illness and how the ECT had affected my memory. The mother related to my story because her sister had once lived with depression. She explained that her sister had suffered for years before finding a medication that helped her. Then she told me the name of that medication.

A couple weeks later, I sat with my doctor in his office trying to choose which medication I would try for a second time. The medication I was taking since ending the ECT was not working. Since my encounter with the man and his mother was still on my mind, I suggested that I try the medication that had helped her sister. Although I had tried this medication before without success, my doctor said it was as good a choice as any. Seven days later I went to a wedding, and... well, you know the rest of the story.

By taking action to find the treatment that will work for you, doors may open that you otherwise would never know existed. In the words of inventor Charles Kettering, "Keep going and the chances are you will stumble on something, perhaps when you are least expecting it. I never heard of anyone stumbling on something sitting down."

The power of *action* is magical, especially when compared to inaction. Until you try any treatment, there is no way of knowing how much it might improve your life. You could be just a few weeks, or even a few days, from ending your struggle with mental illness. The only way you are ever going to know is if you try...

Notes about Chapter Four

Chapter 5
Persistence

Many of life's failures are people who did not realize how close they were to success when they gave up.

—Thomas Edison

Replacing "If..." with "When..."

I first discovered the power of *persistence* by observing my brother-in-law, Scott. I've known him since we were in the sixth grade together, and I can honestly say that I've never met a more persistent person.

I first noticed this quality in Scott when we were in our late teens. He was looking for a job, and decided he would like to work at a store that sold televisions, VCRs, and stereos. Rather than apply at several such stores, Scott aimed his sights on one particular store.

When Scott went into that store to apply for a job, the manager told him that there were no positions available. For most people, this would have been disappointing news. For Scott, it was as if he didn't hear it. The next day, he visited the manager again to see if there were any new openings. The manager told him that there were still no positions available, and he did not expect any for quite some time.

Now, my brother-in-law does not have a hearing impairment. Nevertheless, he went down to that store again the next day... and the next... and the next for about fourteen days straight. Finally, almost in a rage, the manager hired Scott to sweep the floors and do some cleaning for a few hours a day. The manager was impressed with Scott's persistence, and he also wanted to get Scott off his case.

Scott was happy about getting the job, but he really wanted a position as a salesperson. Needless to say, the manager hired him for a sales position just a few weeks later.

A couple years later, after some work in videography, Scott decided he wanted to get into the film business. He wanted to work on film sets making television shows, feature films, and music videos. I suggested it might be easier to become an astronaut, or try to end world hunger. He didn't take my advice.

This is not an easy business to break into, but Scott's persistence paid off again. He learned the names of people in the business, and bugged them for a job. Since he knew very little about the job, he settled for the opportunity just to watch. After a few months of observing, he was eventually asked to help. There was only one catch—he wouldn't be paid. This, of course, was a sacrifice Scott was willing to accept.

Slowly, Scott began getting jobs on the sets of movies, television shows, and music videos that actually paid him for his hard work. It took about a year of free labor before people in the film business accepted him as one of them. Today, Scott lives in Los Angeles and is well-respected in the film business. He has worked on dozens of movies that you have surely seen in the theatres or on video.

Considering Scott's persistent nature, neither the store manager, nor the film industry employers, had

much choice about hiring him. Scott believed he would get the jobs. He took the necessary action to accomplish these goals. *So it was never a question of "if" he would succeed, only "when" he would succeed.* **This is what persistence is all about.**

The Key to Your Prison Window

I hope Scott doesn't take offense to this, but I can't help thinking of him every time I see a housefly. Houseflies have this same unrelenting persistence as they try to find an escape route outside. Have you ever seen a fly trying to get out of a closed window? They keep smacking their little faces into that glass until they either find a hole to get out, or they die from old age. I guess I would do the same if I only had a life span of about one day. Who wants to spend their only day alive stuck in the house?

Are you stuck in the house due to your disorder? Even worse, are you a prisoner of your own mind? I know I was a prisoner of my emotions for thirty-two years. My life was controlled by my mania as well as my depression. Mania caused me to impulsively spend huge sums of money on foolish purchases. I quit jobs with abundant potential to pursue dead-end get-rich-quick schemes. My manic behavior was even responsible for damaging two close friendships I had since childhood.

My depression was no less confining. I lost my incentive to leave the house—even getting out of bed became a chore. I eventually feared socializing. I learned to hate it when unexpected company stopped in at the house. And just the sound of the telephone ringing terrified me as if it was a call from the devil himself.

When your disorder is controlling your life, it has made you its prisoner. The good news is that medical advances of the last decade have provided you with several escape routes. There is no reason to spend the rest of your life stuck on the inside of the window. Surely, you don't want to act less intelligently than a housefly. If not, then you must persist in your treatment efforts until you escape the confines of your brain disorder.

Three Tools for Persistence

Do you know that Abraham Lincoln is believed to have suffered from manic-depression? Whether he did or not, his life is a perfect example of persistence. His story goes like this: In 1831, he failed in business. In 1832, he was defeated for legislature. In 1833, he failed in business again. In 1836, he suffered a nervous breakdown. In 1838, he was defeated for state speaker. In 1840, he was defeated for elector. In 1843, he was defeated for Congress. In 1848, he was defeated for Congress again. In 1855, he was defeated for Senate. In 1856, he was defeated for Vice President. In 1858, he was defeated for Senate again. And in 1860, he was *elected President of the United States.*

I don't think there is a better example of persistence in all of history. I must admit that this story inspired me during my own personal struggle. Imagine the consequences of United States history if Abraham Lincoln had not found the courage to keep trying.

Can you imagine the consequences of your future if you stop trying. That would undoubtedly be a sad story. Now, imagine your future when you succeed at finding the treatment that makes you feel great—day after day. *The first tool for persistence is to* **imagine how your future will be when you get better.**

I had plenty of time to daydream, so I dreamed of how my life was going to be without mania and depression. I visualized Melissa and me laughing and enjoying ourselves while doing all kinds of fun stuff. I pictured us at the big county fair in the fall, in the shopping malls before Christmas, and at the beach in the summer.

I also imagined myself writing a book just like this one. I created a mental picture of myself telling my inspirational story on a talk show like the Oprah Winfrey show. I thought about the millions of patients, as well as their family members and friends, who could benefit from my book. Just the idea that one other person could be saved through my efforts turned my personal struggle to get better into an all-out crusade.

You, too, can imagine how other peoples' lives will change for the better when you find the right treatment. It is easy to think that you and your brain disorder are a burden to others right now, but this way of thinking is self-defeating. You should be focusing on how these people will benefit from your life when you get better. Think about how you will be able to touch the lives of your parents, siblings, children, grandchildren, friends, or other people you know.

Remember the movie, *It's A Wonderful Life*, starring Jimmy Stewart? It's usually televised every year between Thanksgiving and Christmas. This movie is an example of how one person's life affects the lives of everyone they know. By imagining how your successful treatment will not only improve your life, but also the lives of others, you will discover a more meaningful purpose behind your current challenge. This discovery will give you new reasons to persevere.

Whenever my will to persist grew weak, I thought about Melissa. I knew her goals for the future depended on me getting better. We had been together since she was twelve and I was fifteen years old. We had dreams of our future together that had not yet been fulfilled. Furthermore, when my brain disorder became disabling, Melissa became my provider, nurse, therapist, and friend all in one. I wanted to reward her with a life of sunshine and laughter for the selfless sacrifice she gave to me daily. How could I ever reward such love by giving up? Our dreams of the future could only be realized through my ongoing persistence.

*The second tool for persistence is to **focus on what is good in your life, rather than what is bad.*** Above, you learned how to focus on your future; that is, the future you will have when you find the right treatment. Here your focus is on the present; that is, everything that is good in your life today.

The way I focused on everything good in my life was by writing a list. Every day, I made a list of everything I was thankful for in my life. I listed the names of everyone who loved and supported me; the doctor who was trying to help me at the time; the nurses who were kind to me; my cat who comforted me; the books that gave me encouragement and understanding; the television sitcoms that forced me to laugh; the house that sheltered me; the food that fed me; the medication that gave me hope; etc. Anything and anyone I could think of that brought me kindness, happiness, or hope was added to my list.

The key to making this exercise successful is to repeat it every day. Even though you will probably write all the same stuff you wrote yesterday, it is important to start all over again today. Don't look at yesterday's list. By having to think of everything that is good in your life each day, you will help to balance out all those negative thoughts that seem to come so naturally.

If you begin to focus on everything bad in your life, just pick up your list and read it over. It will give you a dose of optimism. If you find this list hard to write, ask someone to help you. As long as you write down everything that *you* can think of first, it can only help to write down additional ideas that didn't occur to you.

The third tool for persistence is to **develop your sense of humor**. This is a tool in which your focus is on the comical and ironic side of life.

Your sense of humor is not dependent on your ability to be happy. Your sense of humor is related to your *perspective*, which is your view of things. Due to your brain disorder, you may have a tendency to view life from a negative perspective. This does not mean you can't change that perspective. With a little practice, you can focus on the lighter side of life. I'm not claiming this will be an easy task. I am promising you, however, that it will make each day an adventure instead of a struggle.

Around the time of my bilateral electroshock treatments, I experienced some temporary memory loss. Some of the things I couldn't remember included: some people's names, directions to places I commonly traveled to, and what kinds of food I normally liked.

One day, while I was pouring Melissa and myself some coffee, she came into the kitchen to talk with me. When she saw me pour cream into both cups of

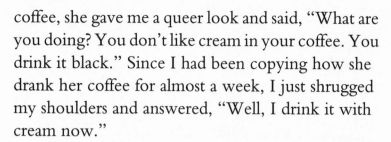

coffee, she gave me a queer look and said, "What are you doing? You don't like cream in your coffee. You drink it black." Since I had been copying how she drank her coffee for almost a week, I just shrugged my shoulders and answered, "Well, I drink it with cream now."

Around that same time, Melissa and I were driving in the car when I pulled over to get us each a hotdog. As I walked up to the hotdog truck, Melissa waited in the car with a silly smile on her face. After I got back, and stuffed the hotdog down my throat, Melissa started laughing and shaking her head in disbelief. "Bob, what are you doing? You hate hotdogs! You haven't eaten one since you were a kid," she said with a giggle in her voice.

Today, I still like cream in my coffee, and I love hotdogs. The point is that some pessimists might have used these events as reasons to focus on why their memory loss is so disturbing. "I don't know who I am anymore!" they might complain. How is this attitude going to help them to persist? I found the whole matter much easier to deal with by seeing the lighter side. There was no harm done, so why not get a chuckle out of it?

I worked at keeping my sense of humor when I experienced side effects from my medication, too. I mentioned the laughter we shared when my muscle twitches caused my arm or leg to hit Melissa while we were sleeping. My friends also teased me when

my slurred speech made me sound like I was imperson-
ating Sylvester Stallone. And you can be sure people
joked about my hair thinning due to one medication,
and about my shaky handwriting due to another.

I'm not trying to make you think that I was the co-
median of the year during my five-year battle with
manic-depression. I definitely was not. I was deeply
depressed. The truth is that while everyone else
laughed about these things, I was often just smiling.
But still, a smile is one thousand times better than a
tear. If I could at least see the humor in the situation,
that was enough to get me through another day
without quitting.

Turning Failure into Stepping Stones

That is basically how I survived five years of failed
attempts in order to discover the one success that
would reward me for the rest of my life. The reality
is that there are no failures. What at first may appear
as a failure turns out to be a valuable stepping stone
toward your goal. This truth is described perfectly in
this quotation from Jacob Riis:

> *"When nothing seems to help, I go and look
> at a stonecutter, hammering away at his
> rock, perhaps a hundred times without as
> much as a crack showing in it. Yet at the*

> *hundred and first blow it will split in two,*
> *and I know it was not that blow that did it—*
> *but all that had gone before."*

I'm going to end this chapter with an anonymous poem that was given to me by my parents during my blackest period of depression. When my father-in-law saw this poem framed on a wall in our home, he told me how this same poem had provided him with the courage to persist during difficult moments in his life. He had two wallet size copies of the poem in his wallet, and he gave one of them to me...

> *When things go wrong, as they sometimes will,*
> *When the road you're trudging seems all up hill,*
> *When the funds are low, and the debts are high,*
> *And you want to smile, but you have to sigh,*
> *When care is pressing you down a bit,*
> *Rest, if you must, but don't you quit.*
> *Life is queer, with its twists and turns,*
> *As every one of us sometime learns,*
> *And many a failure turns about,*
> *When he might have won had he stuck it out;*
> *Don't give up, though the pace seems slow,*
> *You may succeed with another blow.*

Notes about Chapter Five

Chapter 6

Conclusion

Life moves on, whether we act as cowards or heroes. Life has no other discipline to impose, if we would but realize it, than to accept life unquestioningly. Everything we shut our eyes to, everything we run away from, everything we deny, denigrate or despise, serves to defeat us in the end. What seems nasty, painful, evil, can become a source of beauty, joy and strength, if faced with an open mind. Every moment is a golden one for him who has the vision to recognize it as such.

—Henry Miller

Keeping It Simple

Unless a formula for improving your life is easy to use, it isn't worth a cent. That is why my lifesaving formula of *Belief—Action—Persistence* is so valuable. It's simple! In fact, it is so simple that the same concept has been taught in the children's book, *The Little Engine That Could*. Trust that you can do it. Go for it. Never give up until you succeed.

In keeping with this idea of simplicity, I also recommend that you take everything you have read in this book with that idea in mind—keeping it simple. You do not have to do everything the same way I did in order to find the treatment that will end your suffering. There are no strict rules here. You can still get better without having a good sense of humor, without writing a list of everything you are thankful for, and without reading books to learn about your illness. These ideas will help you, but they are not required. If anything I have suggested seems too far of a stretch for you, don't let that worry you. There were plenty of times when I, too, could not always follow the advice I have given in this book.

There were times when I cried about my side effects so long that I made myself sick to my stomach. Sometimes I spent hours dwelling on my pathetic past, or imagining a fearful future. Furthermore, I can assure you that I wasn't thinking of all the good things in my life when I was feeling suicidal.

I Made the Effort— It Changed My Life

The fact is that I am just as human as you. I cried the tears, felt the pain, and knew many of the fears that you probably now know too well. *Still, the point of this book is that I made an effort to change my life. I believed that there was hope for my escape from these horrors of my mentally ill mind, and rather than just wish for my life to change, I struggled to make it happen.* Although depression sucks the energy right out of your mind and body, there are periods of time when the depression loosens its grip. It was during these times that I squeezed out that extra effort to take action toward my goal of mental health.

It was on these days that I chose to laugh, even though it would have been easier to cry. This is when I would make my list of everything that I was thankful for in my life, even though it was easier to find things to complain and whine about. These were also the days when I read books and magazine articles about my brain disorder, and about coping with it, even though it would have been easier to watch television or stare into space.

I never said finding the treatment that will work for you is going to *be* simple. I said you have to *keep it* simple. This means remaining hopeful, going to the doctor, taking your medication or other treatment, and never quitting until you win. That's keeping it simple, and that's all you need to do to find the treatment that will control your brain disorder.

Helping Others Help You

Since finding the energy and motivation to stay focused on the principles of *Belief—Action—Persistence* can be difficult at times, it is extremely important that you share this book with the people in your "support network"—your family, friends, weekly support group members, doctors, therapists, nurses, and anyone else in your life who is trying to help you help yourself.

This book will teach these people in your support network *how* they can best help you. They will learn what you need to be doing in order to get better. Some may be able to provide you with encouragement, while others may be able to give you a ride to the doctor, or remind you to take your medication. These people in your life will learn that they should be helping you focus on the positive aspects of your life, and not just sympathizing with you about the negative. They can also give you a boost toward persistence if quitting becomes one of your options.

As I look back at my time of sickness, I remember some people in my life were very uncomfortable just talking about my disorder. They did not understand it, so they had no idea what to say or do about it. The result was often silence. They hoped that if they ignored it, they wouldn't have to deal with it. The truth, of course, was that they *had* to deal with it, because I was a part of their life, and they were a part of mine.

This book can help the people in your life understand how to act around you. It can relieve the tension that results from their lack of knowledge. Even if they don't quite understand what it is you are feeling, they will at least know how to deal with you. Then, if they want to understand what you are actually feeling, there are countless books in every bookstore that describe the symptomatic behavior you are experiencing. While this book does not explain your disorder in this way, it does explain the three major areas in which a patient needs support.

Three Steps to Unlimited Achievement

There is another benefit your support network, as well as you, will gain from reading this book. This benefit is in learning the *Belief—Action—Persistence* formula, because its power is not limited to the goal of achieving mental health. You can use this formula to achieve any goal in life. Do you want to improve your physical health? Do you want to become financially successful? Do you want to increase your grades in school? Do you want to improve your relationships? The possibilities are limitless with this simple three-step formula.

Let me tell you how I used *Belief—Action—Persistence* in my life after I found a treatment to control my manic-depression. Now that my brain chemicals were balanced, it was time for me to move on with my life. I felt I had gained an upper edge on life with the wisdom and coping skills I had acquired during my time of sickness. Now that my thoughts were clear, I was able to look back in hindsight to recognize how the *Belief—Action—Persistence* formula came into play. Once I recognized it, I knew how to use it for other purposes.

Although I had been out of work on disability for years, I used the formula to overcome my fears and find employment. Within a few months, I used it to start my own business on a part-time basis. And in less than one year, I was self-employed full-time with four people working for my company. I have now had approximately five years of relief from my illness, and there seems to be no challenge that the principles of *Belief—Action—Persistence* cannot overcome.

It is not surprising that each of these three principles are repeatedly the subject of self-help books relating to business, health, finances, education, relationships, and overall psychological well-being. Even though I refer to them as *my lifesaving formula*, it is important that you know that I did not invent *belief, action,* or *persistence*. Each one is a fundamental element of life. Individually, they have incredible power; but together, they can create miracles. That is what they did for me, and that is what they can do for you.

Just Say No to Pessimists

One of the biggest obstacles to your current challenge for mental health may be the limiting opinions of other people. While I recommend that you discuss the issues presented in this book with others, I also warn you that some people have a pessimistic outlook on life and may tell you things that are more likely to hurt you than to help you.

Some people might suggest that you should not get your hopes up—that you should "face the fact" that your brain disorder will handicap you for the rest of your life. The only advice I can offer you is that these people do not know what they are talking about. When it comes to depression and manic-depression, even the best doctors in the world will admit that they can't predict with certainty how any particular patient will respond to a treatment. The message this sends to me is that there is always hope. So don't let anyone tell you differently.

The Only Real Limitation Is the One You Believe

Every year new records are broken. There was a time when nobody thought a human being could run a mile in less than four minutes. Now that someone finally broke that barrier, thousands of other people have been able to do it since that day. The only thing that had stopped the fastest runners in the world from beating that four-minute barricade was the limitation that was in their minds—the belief that it could *not* be done. Finally, when someone proved it could be done, that limiting belief disappeared.

I have written this book so that you will know that it is possible to overcome the painful symptoms of depression and manic-depression. I was suffering as you now suffer. I know depression. I know mania. I know financial stress. I know how difficult these brain disorders are on relationships. I know the tendency to sometimes think that death is the easiest solution to your problems. I understand that there is nothing easy about what I am telling you to do. But I am promising you that there is a light at the end of your dark tunnel, and with what I have revealed to you in this book, you can reach that light as I did.

The Beauty of It All

I can also promise you that life beyond your brain disorder is full of beauty. After you have overcome your disorder, the little problems of everyday life will seem petty and easy to overcome, even though the same problems may seem difficult to other people. You will learn that your brain disorder made you stronger. There will come a day when you will be thankful for your disorder, because it will no longer cause you to suffer, and it will have taught you to appreciate your health.

Today, I appreciate *life* more than most people. I know this is true, because I hear people constantly complaining about life, and I see them oblivious to its beauty. Thanks to my past suffering, I now appreciate even the smallest of life's gifts with tremendous enthusiasm. Today I appreciate smiles, laughter, hugs, full moons, cool breezes, Sunday breakfasts, country drives, nature walks, city skylines, ocean sunsets, soothing music, silence, rain, and an endless list of other treasures that bring me a feeling of blessedness, lifting my spirits to unprecedented heights. I enjoyed all of these gifts before, but not to the degree that I do now.

I recall a *Peanuts* comic strip from years ago that began with Charlie Brown banging his head against a tree. Charlie's friend, Linus, came along and asked, "Charlie, why are you banging your head against that tree?" Charlie's answer was, "Because it feels so good when I stop."

I think this comic strip is illustrating that there is value in human suffering. We can see that Charlie has learned to appreciate a feeling that most of us take for granted. Isn't that what suffering teaches us— appreciation?

Don't we discover a deeper appreciation for all of life's gifts due to some form of suffering? Doesn't death teach, or at least remind us to appreciate others while they are still alive? Isn't our health often taken for granted until we experience sickness? Don't you think that the homeless have a greater appreciation for food and shelter than the wealthy? I know I have a far greater appreciation for mental health, energy, motivation, self-esteem and happiness since experiencing five years of chronic depression.

I don't believe suffering is a necessary prerequisite to learning appreciation, but I do believe that suffering is one vehicle for growth in which our sense of appreciation is enhanced. I find comfort in believing that there is some meaning or benefit behind the illnesses, tragedies, and sufferings of mankind. I have recognized a benefit from my suffering with manic-depression for which I am grateful. I know that there will be a day that you, too, will do the same. (Please reread the Henry Miller quotation at the beginning of this chapter).

Wish You Were Here

Now the rest is up to you. I've shown you that it can be done. I've revealed to you how I did it. I've explained to you how wonderful your life will be when you succeed. If I could do it for you, I would. But that isn't an option. Life insists that you do this on your own so that you can learn the process. Once you use the *Belief—Action—Persistence* formula successfully, it will be yours whenever you need it. So for now, I wish you a fast road to mental health, and a happy balanced life thereafter.

Notes about Chapter Six

Chapter 7

A Message to Your Doctor, Therapist, Counselor, or Nurse

The person who is truly effective has the humility and reverence to recognize his own perceptual limitations and to appreciate the rich resources available through interaction with the hearts and minds of other human beings.

—*Stephen R. Covey*

Dear Doctor, Therapist, Counselor, or Nurse,

Although this book has been written to patients with depression or manic-depression, please do not overlook the assistance it offers to you and other doctors in the mental health care field. The truth is that I originally planned for the message of this book to be the basis of a keynote speech for doctors at medical conventions. I believed that for every doctor who understood the value of my lifesaving formula, *Belief—Action—Persistence*, there would be a hundred or more patients who could benefit from that doctor's knowledge.

After careful consideration, I later realized that a *book* could spread my message faster and farther than *I* ever could giving only one speech at a time. I also decided that it would be more effective to write my book to patients instead of doctors, because doctors will read a book that is written for patients, but patients are less likely to read a book that is written for doctors.

I recently discovered one hitch to my theory. After explaining the subject of this book to a psychiatrist I know, his immediate response was to suggest that I should concentrate my efforts on sharing my message with patients at support group meetings. It was this suggestion that made me realize the need for this chapter.

It is true that the message of this book should be shared with patients and their supporting friends and family members. However, I believe it is just as important for *doctors* to read these pages which I have written. Perhaps the above-mentioned doctor's response is an exception. Perhaps he could not humble himself to accept that a patient with no formal medical education could teach him anything he does not already know.

Considering the possibility that other doctors may make this same assumption, I ask that you give me a few minutes to plead my case. I don't ask this for me, but for the patients whom you treat. It is you, the doctor, who holds the power to turn my simple little book into a means of inspiration, guidance, and hope for all patients. Even more importantly, you are in the most influential position to lead your patients through those three vital steps I have referred to as *belief, action,* and *persistence.*

My expertise in this field comes only from my experience as a patient. Yet this allows you to view your role as a doctor from a new revealing perspective. Since my conclusions have been derived from hindsight, you have the opportunity to survey what actions my doctors took that led to my successful treatment.

Even though you are likely to be familiar with the concept of "my lifesaving formula," it is important in every profession to pause from our routine schedules to remind ourselves of the basics. By reading this book, you are reminded of the omnipotent influence of your words, facial gestures, body language, and overall signs of compassion that you share with each impressionable patient who is depending on your guidance.

If I could emphasize only one idea for you to ponder, it would be that you, and all doctors, have an incredible influence on your patients that places an immense responsibility upon your shoulders. This is the responsibility to provide your patients with hope and the belief that they will get better. This is the responsibility to guide your patients into action by specifically offering them things to do, and more generally, by cheering them on along the way. This is the responsibility to acknowledge the power of your influence in these areas, and to maximize it for your patients' greatest benefit.

In the chapter on *Belief*, I gave some examples of how my doctors influenced me to succeed through that stage. Their heroic influence, however, went far beyond that stage. All my doctors had a great deal of influence on how I succeeded through the *action* and *persistence* stages as well. Let me give you some examples...

When I once missed an appointment with my second doctor, he didn't just let it pass unnoticed. Within two days, I received a letter from him in the mail. The letter stated his concern that I did not show up. It also hinted that I disappointed him for not showing enough interest in my treatment to make the appointment.

This brief letter made a huge statement to me. It said to me that my doctor took my treatment seriously, and that he expected me to do the same. I realized that he did not just show up to my appointments to collect his one hundred and twenty-five bucks. He was there to help me because he thought I wanted his help. Since I really did want his help, I never missed another appointment unless it was absolutely unavoidable.

As another example, when I first conveyed an interest in learning about my brain disorder, my doctors gave me the titles of books to read. If they had the book that they were recommending in their office, they always showed it to me. If they had the time, they also pointed out chapters that might be of particular interest to me. At later appointments, we would talk about the books, and they would answer any questions I had about them.

My doctors also encouraged me to research new medications that were on the market, and we discussed how they might help me. We always talked about the next medication I would try when we realized the one I was using showed no promise. In other words, my doctors didn't just write me a new prescription and hand it to me blindly. They made me feel like I was part of the decision. This is how I was rewarded for taking the action to learn about my brain disorder. They respected me for trying, and their respect influenced me to try more. Plus, this gave me a sense of control over my disorder, and this helped reduce some of the stress that accompanies such a disorder.

Furthermore, my doctors gave me suggestions of ways to help myself. They didn't just ask me how I felt and send me home. They gave me "homework" to do until our next appointment. They suggested I take walks, get out of the house, become a volunteer, or go to support group meetings. I didn't always do these things, but this provided me with options I would not have thought of on my own—like a map with several possible routes to follow.

By emphasizing to you the magnitude of your influence on your patients, I do not mean to place all of the responsibility upon your shoulders. This book has been written to the patient, and the core of its message is about taking responsibility for your own life. Still, in the chapter on *Belief*, I demonstrate that each patient cannot win the battle against depression or manic-depression alone. I follow this up in the chapter on *Action*, explaining that each patient must work *with* their doctor; that is, with the doctor as the guide, while the patient does the work.

In other words, you are not expected to fight each patient's battle against depression or manic-depression by yourself. You are only expected to lead the patient and his supporting troops into battle. That is the aim of this chapter: to remind you of your rank as leader. I am merely one former soldier who is offering you the battle plans of other leaders. That is the aim of this book: to provide you and your patients with the battle plans that led this soldier to victory.

The battle plans I offer are the subject of this book. They are presented as the three-step formula, *Belief—Action—Persistence*. To you, they are a return to basics. To your patients, they are an overview of where they must go to successfully win their battle. It gives them a map to follow. You, as leader, can take what I have given them in simple form, and add detail as needed according to the unique needs of each individual case.

As a final note on getting back to basics, I would like you to remember the reason you chose your career in the first place. If I am correct in assuming that you aspired to change lives and relieve suffering, then my story is one example of that accomplishment. If you get nothing more out of this book than the inspiration to duplicate my story with your own patients, then we have both succeeded.

Notes about Chapter Seven

Chapter 8

Melissa's Message to Those Who Love and Support You

Love cures people—both the ones who give it and the ones who receive it.

—Karl Menninger

Dear Family Member or Friend,

"Is there one thing a person can do to best support a loved one suffering from depression or manic-depression (bipolar disorder)?" This is the question I asked my wife, Melissa, to answer for me as the basis of this chapter on support. If you have read this book, you are already aware of the immense love and support she gave to me while I was struggling with manic-depression. It was her hindsight on this experience that provided her with the insightful answer to my question. This was her answer:

"The best thing that anyone can do to best support someone who is suffering from depression or manic-depression is to learn about the brain disorder. Knowledge is the key to being supportive. Once you learn about the disorder, everything else you need to do to help the patient will come naturally."

How do you get this knowledge? You get it from reading books and magazine articles, attending support group meetings, watching television specials about these brain disorders, and occasionally going to the doctor appointments with the patient. Books are the most convenient sources of knowledge, and there are dozens written specifically about these brain disorders. You will find a list of books related to these disorders in the back of this book.

Melissa explained to me that you can help both the patient *and yourself* by learning about the brain disorder that has affected your lives. Here are a few examples of how your knowledge and understanding of the disorder can *benefit the patient*:

- You can help monitor the patient's progress during treatment by recognizing behavioral patterns or symptoms that the patient might not notice.

- You will have more patience with the patient because you will recognize their undesirable behavior as disorder-related.

- You will be able to help other people in the patient's life become more understanding of the patient's behavior, especially those who are not willing to educate themselves about the disorder.

- You will have a better knowledge of what the patient should and should not be doing so you can *properly* encourage and motivate them toward the most beneficial action.

- You will be one of the few friends or family members the patient can talk to who has an understanding of what they are going through.

- Finally, you can help the patient learn more about the brain disorder while you educate yourself. Learning about the disorder is also one of the best things patients can do to help themselves.

The patient is not the only person who can benefit from your knowledge about the disorder. You, too, can gain tremendously from this education. Your knowledge can free you from the emotional roller coaster ride that comes with trying to support a mentally ill family member or friend. The fact is that it is difficult not to get caught up in the emotions that they are feeling, because it is natural to *react* to their mood swings and related behavior. The greatest reward you can reap from understanding any brain disorder (mental illness) is acquiring the ability to *detach* yourself from the patient's moods and related behaviors.

The following are some examples of the common emotions felt in *reaction* to a patient's disorder-related behavior. These emotions can be eliminated through an educated understanding of the brain disorder:

- **Feeling Anger** (caused by the erroneous belief that the patient's behavior is purposeful.)

- **Feeling Resentment** (caused by the erroneous belief that the patient is to blame for making your life miserable.)

- **Feeling Personally Responsible** (caused by the erroneous belief that you are somehow at fault for the patient's behavior.)

- **Feeling Victimized** (caused by the erroneous belief that you are the target of the patient's behavior.)

- **Feeling Helpless** (caused by the erroneous belief that you have no control over the brain disorder or the behavior that results from it.)

If you have read the chapter on *Belief,* then you know how powerful an effect the above mentioned "erroneous beliefs" can have in your life. These distorted perspectives of reality can be harmful to both the patient and yourself. This is why it is not only helpful, but necessary, that you begin immediately to learn about the brain disorder that is affecting both of your lives.

Finally, your new wisdom will be of great assistance to you when dealing with the ignorant comments of people who know nothing about mental illness, but insist upon giving you their useless advice. The stigma of mental illness is unfortunate, but it is a reality nonetheless. Unless you acquire an understanding of the brain disorder appropriately, you will find yourself naked and vulnerable when the advice of ignorance attacks you. People will suggest tough love and herbal teas, and you won't know what to believe. Before you know it, you might even find yourself questioning the diagnosis. If this occurs, you will be more of an adversary than a supporter.

I have heard it said, "If you are not part of the solution then you are part of the problem." There is some truth to this statement. The question to ask yourself is whether you are an influence on the patient.

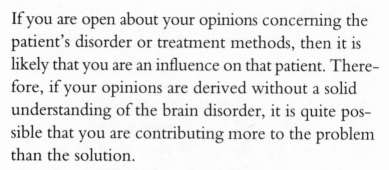

If you are open about your opinions concerning the patient's disorder or treatment methods, then it is likely that you are an influence on that patient. Therefore, if your opinions are derived without a solid understanding of the brain disorder, it is quite possible that you are contributing more to the problem than the solution.

If you want to be part of the solution, then you must learn about the disorder that torments your loved one. It is that simple. As Melissa said, "Once you learn about the brain disorder, everything else you need to do to help the patient will come naturally."

Personally, I believe that anyone willing to make this extra effort for the benefit of another is a hero. There are very few people who will take the time to lift a book or go to a one-hour meeting in order to help another. That is why I hold such admiration, respect, and appreciation for the effort and support my wife gave to me.

Shortly after my five-year struggle with depression had ended, I wrote an essay in tribute to Melissa for the sacrifice she made. I hope it will inspire you to follow her example. I titled this, ***Silent Knights***...

They are heroes, angels and martyrs. Their deeds compare to those of knights in shining armor. But they wear no armor, receive no medals of honor, no trophies, and no promises of reward. They are silent, but they are not unrecognized.

Who are these silent knights? In my life, my wife is one. Her beauty alone guarantees her many choices and opportunities. Her intellect opens many doors. Her personality shines, comforts and heals. Her smile is famous among her peers. Her love is unconditional and unprejudiced. She is blessed with the capability to live any lifestyle she may choose. She chose unselfishly. She chose me.

Five years ago, my wife learned of my mental illness. Our world together was crumbling with emotional and financial difficulties. Yet she never considered escape. She held strong. She provided hope, understanding and unlimited support. We changed roles. She became the pillar upon which I depended. As I slept in avoidance of my hellish thoughts, she became provider, nurse, therapist, friend and lover all in one. At my weakest moments, she also served as my salvation from suicide.

My wife is clearly my knight in shining armor. And yet her deeds were done in silence. Her sacrifice was not in vain. She expected nothing in return. She acted without a selfish thought. She boasted of my successes, but never spoke to her own credit. My struggle for mental health became her struggle. Without any complaint or self-pity, she carried me through five years of combat until my spell of insanity surrendered.

In tribute to my wife and every other silent knight—your deeds may be silent, but they have not been unrecognized. A million thank yous...

Notes about Chapter Eight

Part II

When I wrote this book, I never intended to have a "part one" and a "part two." Part One is the main message about *Belief—Action—Persistence* that originally motivated me to start writing. That is my message of hope and my formula for beating depression and manic-depression that I wanted to share with other sufferers and their supporters.

Yet, when my publisher accepted my book, they asked if there was any additional information I wanted to add to make it longer. So I agreed to add more content.

My original theory was that people who are depressed do not have the energy or motivation to read a long book, and people who are manic do not have the patience. At least this was my experience. This is why I wrote and rewrote Part One over and over until it was as condensed and short as possible. I wanted this book to be simple and easy to read so that everyone, regardless of their mental state, could benefit from reading it.

I did not want to change Part One, so that is why I decided to have a "part one" and a "part two." I have chosen to add five articles that I have written for various purposes over the last year. These are my most popular articles based on the positive feedback I have received from the patients and supporters who have read them.

I now can't imagine this book being complete without them. And since each article stands alone, each can be read at different times and in any order at the pace and liking of each individual reader— thereby putting no pressure on the depressed patient to read them all the way through.

Chapters nine, ten, eleven and twelve offer a valuable perspective on four issues of major importance: labels, masks, suicide, and denial. I believe it will be helpful and enlightening for both patients and supporters to understand these issues from a new revealing viewpoint.

The last chapter, *A Final Message of Hope*, is a short review of my story and message. I wrote it as a concluding inspirational letter for you to pick up and reread whenever you are having a bad day and need your spirits lifted. I sincerely hope it helps. It is true and it is written directly from my heart.

Chapter 9
The Truth about Labels

The truth of it all is that it is just a label. It is not who I am. It is not a reflection of my character. It is not indicative of my intelligence, talents or abilities. It is a label for my doctor to use in treating a chemical imbalance in my brain—period.

—Bob Olson

"Mentally Ill" "Clinically Depressed"
"Manic-Depressive" "Bipolar"

A Categorization of Your Symptoms

What's your label? What does it mean? I remember the psychological stages I went through after being diagnosed with manic-depression. Wow, what a mind trip! At first I began to think that I no longer knew who I was. Had my whole life and identity been a lie? "My God! I'm a manic-depressive!" I even wrote letters to my closest friends and relatives trying to explain my "true" identity, almost apologizing for the lie I had been living.

Finally, I realized the truth behind the labels. Their purpose is to help your doctor know what he/she is dealing with as an illness. After listening to your list of symptoms, your doctor has diagnosed (labeled) you with depression (unipolar disorder) or manic-depression (bipolar disorder). All this label means is that you have a particular group of symptoms. This label now helps your doctor determine what treatment will best relieve you of these symptoms based on the medical community's experience with other patients who have had similar symptoms.

Your label (diagnosis) is nothing more than a categorization of your symptoms. People are not alcoholic or diabetic, they suffer from the symptoms of alcoholism or diabetes. It is not who they are, but rather, the name of the illness from which they suffer.

Remember this the next time you start thinking of yourself as "mentally ill," "clinically depressed" or "manic-depressive."

Extraordinary People Share Your Label

If these labels still make you uncomfortable, just remember that many famous, successful and extraordinary people, past and present, have also been labeled with depression or manic-depression: Abraham Lincoln, Leo Tolstoy, Winston Churchill, Charles Dickens, Vincent Van Gogh, Dick Cavett, Ernest Hemingway, T.S. Eliot, Michelangelo, Bob Boorstin, Rosemary Clooney, Mike Wallace, Irving Berlin, Dick Clark, Emily Dickinson, Sen. Thomas Eagleton, Alma Powell, Hugo Wolf, Jimmy Piersall, Victor Hugo, William Styron, Robert Schumann, Patty Duke, Sylvia Plath, Tennessee Williams, Robert Louis Stevenson, Gov. Lawton Chiles, Walt Whitman, Rod Steiger, Hugo van der Goes, Burgess Meredith, Kristy McNichol and Mike Douglas—to name just a few of the hundreds of well-known people who share these labels with you.

The Secret That Surrounds You

I'll bet you personally know a lot more people than you think you do who have been diagnosed with these labels. I wish more people would open up about

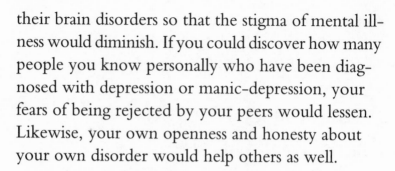

their brain disorders so that the stigma of mental illness would diminish. If you could discover how many people you know personally who have been diagnosed with depression or manic-depression, your fears of being rejected by your peers would lessen. Likewise, your own openness and honesty about your own disorder would help others as well.

Statistics estimate that one out of every ten people suffers from depression or manic-depression. My own experience proves that a much higher number of people have a close relative or friend with one of these brain disorders. There are so many people who need to talk about these disorders with a friend, and they don't even realize that probably one-third of their friends and coworkers have the same need. But our silence condemns us to suffer alone.

When I first started writing about my experiences with my disorder, I was astonished at the number of people who came forward to reveal that they, too, suffered from depression or manic-depression. An even larger number of people came forth to talk about their family members or friends with these brain disorders. In fact, there were very few people Melissa and I would talk to who did not know somebody who had been given one of these labels. But none of these people said anything until they found out that I had manic-depression.

I have a friend who owns a business with about 100 employees. He told me that I was the only person he knew with a mental illness. While visiting his business one day, I randomly gave out free copies of a book I had self-published about these brain disorders to ten of his employees. Within the next week, I was contacted by five of those employees thanking me for the book and describing their own experiences with depression or manic-depression. Three of them had been personally diagnosed, and the other two had family members with these brain disorders. That was five people out of ten—and their employer said I was the only person he knew with a mental illness.

I see this almost daily. I can't even count how many people have told me, in secret, about their depression or manic-depression, exclaiming that they have never told any of their family members or friends about it. It's no wonder people feel so alone and fearful when their doctor diagnoses them with one of these brain disorders. Dozens of their friends and relatives may have the same diagnosis, but everybody's keeping it hidden for fear that they are the only one. And because of their silence, and because of their fear, many people do face their disorder alone.

Stigma V. Support— A Difficult Choice

I'm not suggesting that you should put an announcement in the local paper. I won't deny that the stigma of mental illness exists. I gave up my twelve-year career as a private investigator in order to be open about my illness and write about it. The sad truth is that any lawyer could easily discredit me and my investigation on a witness stand simply by mentioning to a jury that I have a mental illness. One prominent lawyer for whom I handled dozens of investigations even admitted that he could not take the chance of losing a million-dollar case due to the unfortunate reality of this stigma. But that was a price I was willing to pay. It's a choice you have to make for yourself.

I can tell you that I did not lose one friend as a result of my openness—not even an acquaintance. It is also a big relief to be able to talk openly about my disorder and never have to worry about whether people will find out about my "big secret." The truth of it all is that it is just a label. It is not who I am. It is not a reflection of my character. It is not indicative of my intelligence, talents, or abilities. It is a label for my doctors to use in treating a chemical imbalance in my brain—period.

Notes about Chapter Nine

Chapter 10

The Masks We Wear

Since many of us live with our brain disorder for years before being diagnosed, we develop these masks as a tool for coping. And the longer we live with our masks to hide our true feelings, the thicker these masks grow. Before long, we put our masks on automatically, and it takes a conscious effort to take them off—if that is even possible.

—Bob Olson

Our Masks Confuse Our Family and Friends

The other day I talked to a family whose daughter was in a lock-up psychiatric ward due to a suicide attempt. The patient (a young woman in her early thirties) was sitting with her father, mother, and sister in a private visiting room when I arrived there with my wife, Melissa. My first impression when we walked into the room was revealing. The patient, let's call her Julie, was sitting in a chair talking, smiling, and laughing. I immediately identified one of Julie's major obstacles toward achieving the help and support she needed to get better.

Although Julie had experienced prior depressive episodes, as well as prior suicide attempts, this was the first time she had ever stayed overnight at a psychiatric hospital, and the first time clinical depression was ever considered the cause of her suicide attempts. In other words, both Julie and her family were all quite new to this idea that she suffered from a brain disorder called depression. Her prior experiences were blamed on outside causes: adolescence, turbulence in the home, divorce of her parents, etc. Now the truth had made itself known, and the family was lacking in knowledge as to what it all meant.

I knew immediately, as the conversation centered on weather and sports, that Julie hadn't opened up much to her family. How could she? It's like when I talk about the Internet with my father. The lights are on, but nobody's home. Julie was dealing with her family's lack of understanding about her brain disorder the easiest way she could—by putting on her happy face and talking about everything but what she needed to talk about—her depression and her suicide attempt.

This really hit home for me because I was just like Julie when I was depressed. Not everyone is like this, but many patients have learned to get through life wearing a mask to hide their disorder-related symptoms. Since most patients with clinical depression and manic-depression live with their brain disorder for years before being diagnosed, we develop these masks as a tool for coping. And the longer we live with our masks to hide our true feelings, the thicker these masks grow. Before long, we put our masks on automatically, and it takes a conscious effort to take them off—if that is even possible.

I never learned to show my true feelings in front of anyone other than Melissa. If you knew me during my deepest most chronic depression, all you would have seen was an act. I would have appeared happy and full of energy. You would have been very surprised to learn that I was spending about eighteen hours a day during the week sleeping in a depressive coma—partly due to my lack of energy and motivation,

partly due to my need to escape from my hellish and
suicidal thoughts.

Express Verbally What You Are Hiding Physically

Masks are obstacles that we need to acknowledge in
ourselves and explain to other people. The depressed
patient who sits in a chair slumped over with her
eyes focused nowhere does not have to explain to
her family, friends, or doctor that she is depressed.
Her body language explains that pretty well. But the
Julies and Bobs, who mysteriously change from
Jekyll to Hyde depending on who they are with,
have some explaining to do. We have to express verbally what we are not revealing physically.

Doctors understand these masks, but they still have
difficulty seeing past them. It is vital that we look
deep within ourselves to find our true feelings so we
can explain these feelings to our doctors. If we do
not, we may eventually become that patient who is
slumped over with eyes focused nowhere. It does not
have to come to that stage.

Sometimes we become fooled by our own masks.
I remember when I was staying in the hospital waiting
for my first shock treatment (ECT), I began com-
paring myself to the other patients and the way they
interacted with the doctors and nurses. I realized that

I was not like them. No moaning, no groaning. My step was quicker and lighter. I was more polite and friendlier. My conclusion was that I didn't belong there. "There must have been a mistake," I thought. "I shouldn't be getting these treatments. I probably don't even suffer from manic-depression. I'm a liar, a fake!"

Thankfully, a talk with my doctor reminded me of all the evidence. Sure, I wasn't like those other patients. But my life was a mess because of my manic-depression anyway. Everyone is different. We feel many of the same symptoms, but we react to them differently, much the same as we react to different medications in our own unique way. There is no right or wrong way to be depressed or manic. If we have been correctly diagnosed, then we are suffering from one of these brain disorders. We need medical attention. We need help in our own unique way.

A Major Cause for Misdiagnosis

One has to wonder if these masks are not a major cause for misdiagnosis regarding mental illness. I can still remember the faces of some people when I told them of my severe depression. "Perplexed" is the best word that comes to mind. It was obvious they were having difficulty believing that the person in front of them was legally disabled due to depression.

I can only wonder what would have happened if I went to my general practitioner complaining of fatigue,

sore muscles, a loss of appetite, and confusion. How many depressed people who are only able to pinpoint these types of symptoms, and do not understand the signs of mental illness, have been misdiagnosed because of the happy masks they wear on their faces? We will never know.

Open the Lines of Communication

To conclude my story about Julie, my suspicions were correct. She did not know how to start communicating with her mom, dad, and sister; and her family did not know how to respond. Her sister was a little suspicious and confused about the whole situation. She found it difficult to understand how Julie could be depressed to the point of suicide when she appeared so happy and full of life. Our discussion concerning masks brought it all together. Soon we talked about the suicide attempt, and Julie opened up right there in front of her family, even with her mask still on. Good job, Julie! Now the lines are open. Let's hope the communication keeps flowing both ways.

If you have a mask that you put on when you are around other people, remember to explain it to your doctor and those who support you. Always be truthful about your symptoms verbally, even if your mask won't reveal them physically.

Notes about Chapter Ten

Chapter 11
The Mystery of Suicide

...I know I never wanted to die. I only wanted relief from my depression.

—Bob Olson

Inappropriate Reactions to the Talk of Suicide

Very few people like to talk about suicide. It is one of those subjects that instantly fills your stomach with a feeling of panic and fear. However, not talking about suicide can be a dangerous problem. I know all too well because I kept it hidden for much too long while I was suffering from chronic depression. Later, when I really needed help, Melissa was hearing the word for the first time. Because she was not used to me talking about it, she instantly got scared. I sensed her fear and I froze up—immediately trying to cover up by making light of the subject. The problem escalated until I finally talked to my doctor about it. Thankfully, I didn't wait until it was too late.

Melissa eventually became my best listener because she made an effort to learn about suicide. Today I realize that she just needed to understand a little more about it to be comfortable with the subject. Originally, she felt *responsible* to hear that I was having suicidal thoughts. She also felt *hurt* that I wanted to leave her. What is surprising to most people is that these reactions are quite inappropriate, although they come to us most naturally.

People attempt and commit suicide for different reasons. However, in reference to clinical depression and manic-depression (bipolar disorder), I believe many patients will relate to my own experience...

A Desperate Need to Escape

For me, suicide was not so much a selfish act as it was a means of escape. There were times in my life when my depression became so painful and tormenting that I was unable to think rationally. My ability to see any hope that I would ever get better was temporarily disabled. All I could see and feel was the black hole which surrounded me. I felt as if I must be partially dead already. So with these thoughts, and because my judgment was impaired, my only hope for escape from it all was a bullet in my brain. I was unable to imagine a more promising option for escape from my suffering.

The point I wish to make is that I was unable to see beyond my pain. The problem that occurs in this state of mind (severe depression) is that we can't see beyond the suffering to even think about others. We have lost hope and we are looking for an escape from our living hell—a quick solution to our problems. We are unable to recognize these problems as temporary and our solution as permanent. Our problems and fears have been blown out of proportion by a mentally ill mind, and we feel cornered by a demon we think we cannot conquer.

I am still here, so I obviously never committed suicide. I'm not sure if I ever attempted it, although I put a gun to my head more than once. I vividly remember the rattling of the steel barrel against my teeth as I held the gun in my mouth. So I guess that is as close to an attempt as I ever want to get. Still, I know I never wanted to die. I only wanted relief from my depression.

Suicidal Thoughts—My "Get Out of Jail Free" Card

I had "suicidal thoughts" for most of my life. These were more like a death wish than an intent to kill myself. I told my doctors about them, and they were naturally quite concerned. They became even more concerned when I explained that I owned a gun, and that I knew I would use that gun if I were ever going to take my own life. But I always saw my suicidal thoughts as helpful. As strange as that may sound to some people, it made perfect sense to me. And I know other people suffering from depression who agree with me.

My suicidal thoughts actually comforted me because they promised me a means of escape if the pain became too severe to handle. In other words, they provided me with an option that would always be there if I needed it. I could be having the toughest day of my life, my mind could be pounding me with exaggerated fears and self-defeating messages, and as painful as it all was, I knew that if it escalated to the point where I could take it no more, I always had the option to kill myself. The thought of suicide was my "get out of jail free" card, and it was strangely comforting to know it was there.

For me, thoughts of suicide worked as my coping mechanism. When life grew difficult, and my clinical depression made all my problems ten times worse than they actually were, I always told myself, "If it gets unbearable, I can always commit suicide tomorrow, but for now I'll just stick it out another night."

Unfortunately, there is a fine line between suicidal thoughts and a suicide attempt. Such thoughts are a severe symptom of depression that you must talk about with your doctor in order to diagnose and treat your brain disorder properly. Thoughts of suicide represent the type of distorted thinking that is common with clinical depression. All suicidal thoughts are a serious threat, and you should never handle such a crisis alone—even if you think your thoughts of suicide are just a coping mechanism. The symptoms of depression prevent us from being able to know the difference between a serious threat and a coping mechanism.

Suicidal Thoughts Are a Serious Symptom of a Serious Disorder

For the patient who has suffered most of his/her life with depression or manic-depression, suicidal thoughts may seem like a normal occurrence. I recall a talk I was having with a friend just months after I had found a medication that worked for me. He was telling me that he often had thoughts of suicide. He had never attempted to kill himself, but he thought about it often. I had only been well for a few months, so I responded to him by saying I believed everyone had these thoughts. I knew that I did. I couldn't imagine a life without them.

About a year-and-a-half later, I was sitting in my kitchen talking with Melissa about how lucky I was to be better. I came to the momentary realization that I had not experienced a suicidal thought in almost two years. As I told Melissa about this discovery, my conversation with my friend popped into my head. "Oh my God, Melissa! I have to make a phone call," I told her. And I ran to the phone to contact my friend.

I told my friend that suicidal thoughts are not normal. I told him how wonderful life feels without them. I told him that if he was still thinking about suicide, that he should see a doctor immediately. My friend told me to relax because he had been seeing a psychiatrist for about a year. He said that I no longer needed to worry because he had conquered his demons months ago. I immediately burst with a sigh of relief.

If you suffer from thoughts of suicide, inform your doctor immediately. If you know you are contemplating suicide, seek help from your doctor, a friend, and/or a family member without delay. Don't be wishy-washy about it, either. Tell them right out that you are in a desperate state of mind, and your thoughts continue to focus on suicide. I know from experience that you cannot talk yourself out of this state. Get help right away!

For the loved ones who are trying to understand suicide, I hope this helps to change your perception of it. By understanding suicide in this way, you can release your feelings of guilt and hurt, and begin seeing suicide for what it is—a serious symptom of a serious brain disorder.

Understanding the brain disorder (mental illness) from which your loved one suffers is vital if you want to support them. Suicide is one aspect of mental illness that screams for your understanding and attention. When a person is suffering so severely that they are considering taking their life to stop their pain, they need professional attention fast. Do not take it lightly. Calmly call a psychiatrist or a psychiatric hospital (found at most large medical hospitals), or at least call your local hospital emergency room for immediate professional attention.

The bottom line is that this is such an important subject for both patients and supporters to understand, that everyone needs to educate themselves about it. Melissa is the most supportive human being on this earth, yet she was unable to talk to me about my suicidal thoughts until she understood suicide better by reading about it in books and talking about

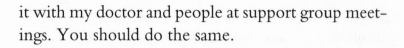

it with my doctor and people at support group meetings. You should do the same.

Suicide Prevention Should Begin before a Crisis Occurs

Suicide prevention should take place before a crisis occurs. This means that you should begin communicating about this subject today, whether it is an issue or not. If you are a patient with depression or manic-depression, you need to know that you have someone to go to when you have suicidal thoughts. If you are a supporting friend or family member, you need to discuss suicide with your suffering loved one now, so that this person knows they can go to you if they begin to experience suicidal thoughts in the future.

Now would also be the best time to discuss the subject of suicide with your doctor and therapist. Both patients and supporters should prepare ahead of time so that nobody panics if the time comes when the patient needs to discuss his suicidal thoughts. A plan to contact your doctor or hospital should be in order.

The goal here is for the patient to have a relationship with someone whom they won't hesitate to talk to about their suicidal thoughts due to fear, guilt, or embarrassment. The person suffering with these suicidal thoughts believes he has run out, or is close to running out, of treatment options that will end his pain.

What he needs is hope that a better alternative is available—hope that he can and will get better if he just keeps on fighting and persisting in his treatment efforts.

The best way to restore this hope is by listening to the patient. Let the person verbalize their immediate fears and feelings that are causing them this horrible pain and these unbearable thoughts. After they have fully explained why they wish to die, each one of those issues needs to be discussed—in a nonconfrontational manner.

The patient needs to know that his fears and his pain are only the result of his depression. Then he needs to be reminded that his depression is treatable; and he needs to relearn what is being done to treat it. He also needs to be reminded of how much better and happier his life will be without the depression. And finally, he needs to be told that he is loved and needed.

My doctors were brilliant in handling my suicide issues because they made sure that I did not leave their care without a new vision of hope that I would soon beat my brain disorder. If I was convinced that the medication I was trying was not helping, they would either restore my faith in that medication by reminding me that the medication needed more time to work in my system; or if that did not work, they would actually change medications or add another treatment to the formula.

Any one of these methods would normally provide me with new hope that I could take with me to ward off my suicidal thoughts. I thank each and every one of my doctors for continuing to do this throughout my five-year battle with manic-depression. I also thank my wife, Melissa, for always listening to me, showing me that I was loved and needed, helping me see past my distorted thoughts, and restoring my hope on a daily basis.

I must remind you that I am not a doctor. I am sharing this information based on my own experiences only. Not every patient is going to be just like me. That is why it is so important to contact a doctor about suicidal thoughts, preferably a psychiatrist who specializes in depression and manic-depression. Only a trained and experienced professional can know the best way for you to handle this issue.

For more information on the value of hope, please reread the section on hope in Chapter Three.

Notes about Chapter Eleven

Chapter 12

The Trickery of Denial

*I was blind to the truth because I could only see
what I wanted and expected to see...
...I might have saved myself months or years
of suffering.*

—Bob Olson

Looking for Evidence of a Disorder

Before I was first diagnosed, I called a psychiatrist for an appointment because I knew there was something wrong with me. Prior to going to that appointment, Melissa and I sat down for hours writing a list of all the unusual behavior, feelings, and emotions I had experienced in the past. We wanted to tell the doctor about everything on this list so she would have plenty to go on when she diagnosed me. At that time, we were looking for evidence of a disorder, so we were able to see the signs.

My doctor diagnosed me with manic-depression and immediately put me on Lithium. Melissa and I raced to the bookstore to buy all the books my doctor had recommended. After reading them, we felt we understood the brain disorder and how to identify its symptoms. We thought we were prepared for anything. Unfortunately, we were not prepared for what was to come.

After being diagnosed, I was relieved to learn that my painful and destructive past behavior was due to a chemical imbalance in my brain. I was even more excited to learn that this chemical imbalance could be controlled with medication. It was great news, but I didn't know what to expect. Since I had lived with manic-depression since childhood, I didn't know what it would feel like without it. All I could go by was my own expectations of what that would be like.

Looking for Evidence That I Was Better

I wanted to believe that the Lithium was working for me. I wanted it so much that I convinced myself that I was feeling better than ever. Whenever someone asked me how the medication was working, I said, "Great! I've never felt better." And every time I said it, I believed it even more. By this time, I was no longer looking for evidence of my disorder. Instead, I was only focused on evidence that I was better, and I refused to see anything else.

Four months later, in the dead of a New England winter, I was crying to Melissa about how empty I felt inside. I convinced her and myself that my inner pain was due to my job and my surroundings. I had already convinced us that the Lithium was working, so I had to blame my depression on outside sources. "If I can just move to Los Angeles and get a new job, then everything will be better," I told her. And I was so sure of it that I convinced her and everyone I knew that this was a good idea.

Well, we did move to California. But to make a long story short, that didn't solve my problem. The fact is that I had been falling deeper and deeper into a depression all the time I was taking Lithium. Unfortunately, this particular medication did not work for me even though it has worked for millions of other patients. So by the time we got out to Los Angeles, I was so deeply depressed, lethargic, and socially withdrawn that getting a job was not as easy as I had expected.

Actually, I did get one job. But I had to quit when I was so upset that my boss wouldn't buy a coffee maker for customers to use in the waiting room that I started crying. Obviously that is not why I started crying, but I couldn't see the truth at the time. I was in denial that the Lithium was not working for me, and I was unwilling to accept that I still suffered from my brain disorder. In short, I was very confused.

The Blindness of Expectation

The moral of this story is that we are all vulnerable to the trickery of denial, or, as I call it, "the blindness of expectation." I was blind to the truth because I could only see what I wanted and expected to see—that the Lithium was working for me and that I no longer suffered from manic-depression. If I had just allowed myself to recognize that I really did not feel any better on the Lithium, I might have saved myself months or years of suffering. I definitely would have saved Melissa and myself a long difficult journey to California and back.

How to Recognize the Signs

If you find yourself making big changes in your life, you should look closer at the motive behind each one. It could be a job change. It could be a move to another city or state. It could be a relationship change. Even just moving to another house or apartment, or buying a new car, might be a sign that you are suffering inside but are blaming your pain on outside circumstances.

Of course, just one job change or relationship change does not mean there is definitely a problem. However, if you have been diagnosed with depression or manic-depression, I am just warning you that such a life change could be a red flag waving at you to be noticed. Certainly, if you have made many changes in your life, you should think twice about the underlying reason behind them all—especially if you had hoped these changes would eliminate some painful or empty feeling within you, but they didn't. Maybe the source of your painful or empty feeling is really an internal problem that should not be blamed on external circumstances.

Don't expect your doctor to notice these signs. My doctor never suspected a problem when she learned of my plans to move across the country. Despite the fact that I was giving up a lucrative business, had never been to Los Angeles, and was moving out there without a clue as to where I would live or work, my doctor never suggested there might be a hidden motive behind it all. Why not? Because I was so convinced that the Lithium was working, that I convinced her of it, too. If you find it hard to understand how I could do that without her noticing, make sure you read my chapter on masks.

Melissa and I lived in Los Angeles for almost a year. Despite being an ambitious person by nature, I only worked a few weeks during the entire time we lived there. From the day we moved there until the day we left, my symptoms intensified: I cried without cause, I became more socially withdrawn, I began sleeping most of my days away, I became weak and thin, and my thoughts increasingly focused on suicide. All this was evidence of major depression, yet nobody could recognize the cause of my suffering because I would not allow it. I was no longer looking for signs of a disorder. I was looking for signs to prove what I had expected from the Lithium—that it was making me feel better.

Take Responsibility for Your Own Mental Health

Finally, after we moved back to New England, my doctor recognized what had happened. It was a bit obvious when I called her to explain the horror of my persistent suicidal thoughts and the dreadful story of my year in California. Still, it was not her fault. It was nobody's fault except my own. Regardless of the signs, I refused to see that I was still depressed. Not until my depression had escalated to the point where I was totally disabled and dangerously suicidal did I finally admit that the Lithium was not working.

It does not have to reach this extreme for you. Be aware of the signs—both the easy-to-recognize and the not-so-obvious. My problem was not the Lithium. Lithium has helped millions of patients beat their illness. It just didn't work for me. My problem was in my inability to admit that the Lithium was not working. This denial caused me to fall into such a deep depression that it required twenty-one shock treatments to pull me out of it. I hope you can learn from my mistake.

Notes about Chapter Twelve

Chapter 13

A Final Message of Hope

Have hope,
succeed with hope,
and then give hope to others.

—Bob Olson

If I had to sum up the message of this book in one word, I'd have to say it's a message of "hope." I believe that hope is a magic ingredient for any treatment program that has the power to save lives. For me, hope that I would one day find a treatment to end my suffering was what kept me from taking my own life during my darkest depths of depression.

I am so thankful today that I was able to remain hopeful, no matter how faint that hope may have been at times, because I no longer suffer from the painful symptoms of bipolar disorder. In fact, I have been free of all manic and depressive symptoms since September 1994. Although I will always have my brain disorder, I now control it rather than it controlling me. That is why I can say that I have truly beaten my disorder.

My message of hope to you is a simple one. No matter how dismal life may seem to you now, know that you can find a way to beat your brain disorder (mental illness). Know that your depression and mania are only a chemical imbalance in your brain and not a character flaw. Your disorder is a biologically based physical disorder just like Alzheimer's disease, Parkinson's disease and epilepsy. It affects you psychologically as well as physically, but it is a chemical imbalance in the brain that is treatable.

You may remember from Chapter Two that I experienced mania and depression ever since I was a child. However, I was not diagnosed with bipolar disorder until I was twenty-seven years old. I sought help for my disorder because the symptoms intensified and became too obvious to ignore. My diagnosis was an easy one, but finding a treatment that worked for me was not so easy. It took over fifteen failed medications (and combinations thereof), twenty-one ECT (electroconvulsive therapy) treatments, three doctors, two ECT specialists, and five years to finally end my suffering.

There are many people who have suffered more than me, and many who have found the right treatment on their first or second trial. My point is not to compare sad stories, but to inspire success stories. I want you to know that success did not come easy to me so you understand that even those with stubborn cases can get better. This is important knowledge because the key to finding a treatment that works for you is summed up in one word—*persistence*. Never give up trying!

If I had given up after my first failed medication, or my fourth, or my tenth, or even my fifteenth... If I had given up after my eighth shock treatment (ECT), or my thirteenth, or my twenty-first... If I had given up trying anywhere along the way, before I finally found that one treatment to save me, I would not be the happy healthy person I am today. I would not be running my own successful business. I would not have been able to write this book and become a published author. I would not appreciate every waking moment. I may not even be alive.

What I want you to know is that there is a treatment for everyone who suffers from depression and manic-depression (bipolar disorder). The sad truth is that there is not just one treatment that works for every case. That makes some people's battle with their brain disorder difficult—but not impossible. If you run out of options because you have tried every treatment on the market, I have good news for you.

First, there are new treatment alternatives constantly becoming available to us. And second, the medication that finally worked for me was something that I had already tried once before without success.

My doctors believe that the ECT (electroconvulsive therapy) actually pulled me out of my severe depression so that the medication could take over from there. I didn't realize it at the time because I did not recognize any significant improvement from the ECT. But when I retried the medication that had previously failed me, it was evident that the ECT had an effect. This is encouraging because it is evidence that success is still possible even if we have run out of new options to try.

Can you imagine how I felt when my doctor told me that, aside from the twenty-one ECT treatments, I had tried every category of medication that existed at that time, and my only hope was to start trying them all over again? You probably can imagine that my hopes were a bit deflated. Deflated, yes. Totally hopeless, no way.

I constantly reminded myself that millions of unipolar and bipolar patients have beaten their brain disorders. Now I can add my name to that list. There is no reason to think that you are any different. Hey, my doctors had even labeled me "medication resistant." If that's not a pin in the hope balloon, I don't know what is. What matters, though, is that I did not accept negative messages from negative people. And today I am rewarded with happiness, mental health, and stability.

For your own sake, do not listen to anyone who tells you that you can't get better. I promise that if you just keep trying, you will add your name to our list of those who have found mental health. With persistence, you are sure to find the treatment that will totally, and unbelievably, change your life forever.

If this sounds like a pep talk, maybe it is. It may be the most important pep talk of your life. There are not many of us who wish to look back at our painful past in order to root others across the finish line. Some people simply want to forget about their mental illness and pretend it isn't there. Others are trying to hide it due to its stigma. But I want to remember and share my story, because that is what I needed when I suffered.

I remember wishing for such a pep talk when I was in your shoes. I lived for it. I searched the bookstores for inspiration—any reason to go on for one more day. And so I tell my true story so that some of you will hear my simple message of hope: "If I did it, then so can you."

I hope that you will share your inspirational story with others after you find the treatment that ends your suffering. Meanwhile, please share my message of hope with others so that they, too, will see that there is a light at the end of their dark tunnel of suffering. And give praise to the supporters—the pillars upon which we lean—who keep us alive with their love and selfless sacrifice. May we, as patients, learn from them so that we may make the transition from sufferer to supporter after we have found our own mental health. In simpler words: have hope, succeed with hope, and then give hope to others.

Warmest Regards,

Bob Olson

Resources

National Mental Health Association

Information Center
1021 Prince Street
Alexandria, VA 22314
1-800-969-NMHA

(contact for information on available resources)

National Alliance for the Mentally Ill

200 North Glebe Road, Suite 1015
Arlington, VA 22203-3754
1-800-950-NAMI

(newsletter, mailing list; call for referral to group nearest you; annual convention in Chicago)

National Institute of Mental Health

Public Inquiries
5600 Fishers Lane, Room 7C-02
Rockville, MD 20857
1-800-421-4211
(call for list of free publications)

National Depressive and
Manic-Depressive Association

730 North Franklin Street, Suite 501
Chicago, IL 60610
1-800-82-NDMDA
(membership organization, direct support, advocacy, litigation, public awareness, education)

American Psychiatric Association

APA Department MH
1400 K Street NW
Washington, DC 20005
1-202-682-6220
(referrals to obtain physicians who specialize in the diagnosis and treatment of mental illness)

Books about Depression and Manic-Depression

Overcoming Depression. Demitri F. Papolos, M.D. and Janice Papolos. HarperCollins, 1997. (Detailed and informative but easy to understand. My number one recommendation—I love this book. This is one of the books that helped me most when I was suffering.)

Understanding Depression. Donald F. Klein, M.D. and Paul H. Wender, M.D. Oxford University Press, 1994. (I also highly recommend this book because it helped me when I was suffering. The brilliance of this book is that it turns a complicated brain disorder into something that is easy to understand. Everyone should have this book.)

Manic-Depressive Illness. Frederick K. Goodwin and Kay Redfield Jamison. Oxford University Press, 1990. (More of a medical textbook, but still fairly easy to read.)

A Brilliant Madness: Living with Manic-Depressive Illness. Patty Duke and Gloria Hochman. Bantam Books, 1993. (Biography of Patty Duke's life with manic-depression, plus informative medical information.)

The Depression Workbook: A Guide for Living with Depression and Manic-Depression (1992); and *Living without Depression and Manic-Depression: A Workbook*

for Maintaining Mood Stability (1994). Mary Ellen Copeland. New Harbinger Publications. (Both books are informative with helpful workbook format exercises.)

Moodswing. Ronald R. Fieve, M.D. Bantam Books, 1997. (Detailed and informative.)

An Unquiet Mind: A Memoir of Moods and Madness. Kay Redfield Jamison. Alfred A. Knopf, 1997. (Autobiography of Jamison's experience with her manic-depression.)

The Pill Book. Harold M. Silverman, Ed. Bantam Books, 1998. (Just the facts about medications; found in most pharmacies. Most any book about medications will do, but every patient should have one.)

Ask at your favorite bookstore or library for a complete list of available books about depression and manic-depression (bipolar disorder).

Index

A

action, 34–35, 40–42
anger, 82
antidepressant drugs, 16, 28
appointments, medical, 36, 74–75
appreciation, 52, 66–68
art, as therapy, 38

B

belief, 24–25, 27–31, 35
Belief—Action—Persistence formula, 11, 39, 63–65, 68–69
beliefs, limiting, 6–8, 65–66
blindness of expectation, 120
Brown, Charlie, 67

P

painting, as therapy, 38

Peanuts, 67

persistence

  examples of, 16–21, 46–48, 55–56, 127–30

  tools for, 50–55

personal responsibility, taking

  for the patient's behavior, 82

  for your own mental health, 122–23

pessimism, 65

photography, as therapy, 38

R

religion, 39

resentment, 82

responsibility, personal. *See* personal responsibility, taking

Riis, Jacob, 55–56

S

sculpture, as therapy, 38

self-education

  for family members and friends, 80–84, 106, 111–12

  for patients, 37–38, 75

sense of humor, developing a, 53–55

side effects, medication, 17–18, 54–55

Silent Knights, 84–85

simplicity, 60–62

spiritual action, 39

suffering, 66–68